The Wit
of Peter Ustinov

For
The Bishop of Limpopoland,
Madame Liselotte Beethoven-Finck
and, of course, for
Peter Ustinov

The Wit
of Peter Ustinov

Compiled by
Dick Richards

LESLIE FREWIN : LONDON

Also by Dick Richards:
The Curtain Rises . . .
Wiv a Little Bit of Luck
(in collaboration with Stanley Holloway)
The Wit of Noël Coward

First published 1969 by
Leslie Frewin Publishers Limited,
One New Quebec Street, Marble Arch, London W1

This book is set in Bembo,
printed by Anchor Press
and bound by William Brendon,
both of Tiptree, Essex

World Rights Reserved
09 096310 5

CONTENTS

Introduction

Bulky, brilliant Peter Ustinov, who sometimes looks like the Chairman of the Board of Directors of a bunch of talented gnomes, wears many hats and, though only in his late forties, can justly wear them at the slightly jaunty angle which denotes success.

Take a deep breath.

He is a playwright, actor, director, screenwriter, producer, novelist, short-story writer, journalist, lecturer, television and radio personality, star of several discs, producer of an opera, cartoonist, linguist, *bon viveur*, mimic, world traveller, avid student of world affairs and music, and Rector of Dundee University.

He is also – this intelligent, well-read cosmopolite – a family man, a 'mucker-about' with boats, a compulsive motorist and no mean opponent at tennis.

More important is that he follows these varied paths with panache, energy and excited zeal; the day to him consists of twenty-four hours of golden interest waiting to be minted. Even when he relaxes, and this he has been known to do, he does it with style and completely fulfilled contentment.

Yes, Ustinov is one of the more remarkable young men of our age.

His varied activities have led to an assortment of awards.

He has won two 'Oscars', a 'Grammy', and two 'Emmies' for the best American television performance on an Omnibus

TV show, when he portrayed Dr Johnson. He has earned two Academy nominations, the American Donaldson Award for the best play by a new author (that was a few years back), the London *Evening Standard* Drama Award, nominations for the Antoinette Perry Award for the Best Play and the Best Performance on Broadway, the David O Selznick Silver Laurel Award in Germany for his film, *Billy Budd*, and eight nominations for the British Film Academy 'twin-brother' of the 'Oscar'.

Outstandingly, he was the first actor to be awarded the Benjamin Franklin Medal presented by the Royal Society of Artists for his 'notable contribution to the arts'.

Ironically, there is no official award for the Wit of This (or any other) Year, or he would be a sure contender.

This little book is an attempt to bring some of that wit between hard covers. Don't think that it has been an easy task; it has been fraught with difficulties.

Keeping abreast with Ustinov is a problem, for, by jet, boat, train, car and, for all I know, by cycle, caravan, or camel, he is invariably going somewhere other than the place you expected to find him. When he stays put he is courteously and genially approachable. But when does he stay put?

So one spends the intervals between seeing him in reading everything he publishes (rewarding in itself), seeing his plays and talking with his many friends. But his wit is so often buried in wisdom and cannot always readily be mined for the nuggets essential for a book such as this.

His friends confirm what one knows; that his wit is not that of the 'I say, I say, a funny thing happened to me on the way to the theatre', but a more mellow and more profound approach, based on the art of the raconteur which, in turn, is based on mimicry, acting ability, command of tongues and accents and astute observations of places, people and their peccadilloes.

I have on my desk a large file of letters from Ustinov's friends and admirers who, while not always able to supply sparkling *bons mots*, graphically grapple with the task of joyfully describing incidents and situations, how he visualised them and brought a succession of eccentrics to uncanny life.

Ask him, for example, to describe how a German tourist would face the Mexican Customs while carrying 1,000 grains of heroin and being ogled by an Italian harlot from a nearby hotel.

No, it is not easy to crystallise the agile wit of a Ustinov but I hope the attempt is worthwhile.

I recall interviewing him once at the London Hilton Hotel when he was hastily dressing to keep a lunch date (which he claimed had slipped his mind) with Queen Elizabeth, the Queen Mother. As he clambered into a slightly creased dark suit and pulled on a pair of highly cosiery gent's hosiery (for Beau Brummel he is NOT) he patiently and accurately answered my questions and coped with a ringing telephone even though the hour of the Royal date was perilously near.

Later I was emboldened to write to Her Majesty and ask if, during that lunch, she remembered him making any witty remark which might be useful grist to my mill.

Her Private Secretary courteously replied that 'Mr Ustinov was his usual charming and amusing self but in the general flow of conversation it was not, I am afraid, possible for the Queen Mother or himself to pinpoint anything of particular wit which I can regale to you.'

Reading between the lines of this consummately tactful letter I still have a hunch that Ustinov probably 'stopped the show' once or twice during that luncheon party.

Anyway, I regard the Queen Mother's comment as a most gracious Royal accolade. A considerably more significant and revealing Royal nod, for instance, than the Beatles' 'gong.'

Dick Richards

The Father of the Man

Peter Ustinov comes of artistic, comfortably placed, polyglot stock. As a child and youth he was intelligent, impressionable and vitally curious, three qualities that have never deserted him. Many of his views on family life and education spring from his early days.

Education is important, especially in alleviating prejudice. If you are going to be a prisoner of your own mind the least you can do is to make sure that your cell is well furnished.

My father was an extraordinary man when it came to money. He somehow managed to live all his life with the gusto and philanthropy of an extremely wealthy man – without being burdened with the many complications of actually possessing any money.

I have never quite recovered from the psychological impact of a school report I received which I would not have believed possible had my mother not shown it to me. It read: 'This boy shows great originality, which must be curbed at all costs.'

11

At school we had to wear a top hat and tail-coat and carry a furled umbrella. The school prospectus said the umbrellas were essential to differentiate us from City of London bank messengers.

Any child worth his salt will learn more by reaction against than obedience to.

Education is not confined to school. It continues relentlessly to the end of life.

I was quite a nice child, I think, except that when other children misbehaved I gather they were threatened with me as a playmate.

British education is probably the best thing in the world if you can survive it; if you can't there's nothing left for you but the diplomatic corps.

When I was a child I used to play a flute, not because I loved it, but because there was a shortage of flautists in the school orchestra.

I've got rather a large upper lip; consequently when I played the flute I very often got the right notes but invariably got the wrong octave. Somehow, in Handel's *Messiah*, this fault stood out.

I certainly miss some things from school, enormously at times. Like that odious custard, and that shepherd's pie, so horrid. Yet I occasionally have great nostalgia to taste it again, rather, I suppose, as a criminal returns to the scene of his crime.

School is only the place where you learn to learn. So it becomes a useful pastime at a period of life when the mind needs such a pastime.

When I was twenty we did not have the cult of the teen-ager and there was no particular merit in being twenty. At that age I had my first play produced and it was considered an impertinence rather than a phenomenon.

*   *   *

He was not apparently a distinguished scholar at either his prep. school or Westminster public school:

Because I had a German passport, at school I was always regarded with some suspicion as the boy who lost the last war.

*   *   *

Ustinov as a 'Youthful Prodigy':

One of my earliest 'triumphs' was to win a school poetry competition with a piece of satirical material which sounded like something that A P Herbert might have tossed off at the age of two while standing, as a punishment, in Patience Strong's Corner.

*   *   *

One of his schoolmates at Westminster was the son of German Ambassador von Ribbentrop. Says Peter:

Young Ribbentrop had been refused, I believe, at Eton, which meant that he automatically came to us at Westminster, where the clothes were similar, but the reputation not quite so giddy and with much smaller playing fields on which battles could be won or lost.

*   *   *

When asked at prep. school, on the first day, where he wanted to sit, young Ustinov diffidently muttered 'At the back!':

I have since been forced to moderate this highly laudable sentiment.

*   *   *

Enlarging on his mixed blood, Ustinov told David Clayton:

I claim an Arab uncle by marriage and, further, a mistake

by a Lutheran pastor in Württemberg at my christening made me for half an hour a full-blooded German baby with the names of Horst Willibald Otto. Another child was given the name Peter and sprinkled with Jordan water (which at my grandmother's request had been brought to Württemberg in a corked hot water bottle); I, in turn, was christened Horst and received nothing!

* * *

He sums up his bizarre family background by stating:

Without a drop of English blood I was born an Englishman.

* * *

His love of eccentric and exotic motor-cars goes back to his childhood:

I used to be a motor-car. I was six and sheer hell to live with. I switched myself on in the morning and drove myself around all day, backing through doors, purring away. I remember my mother once had bad toothache and I tried to drown her moans by revving up on my 'motor'. She shouted at me to stop. My grandfather protested. 'You should not talk that way. That is his imagination developing.'

* * *

Ustinov's father, a journalist, is a vivid character in Peter's mind.

In Geoffrey Willans' biography of Ustinov, Peter recalls:

My father started hundreds of novels but never, ever, got past the first page. I don't think he ever quite forgave me when my first play was produced, not because I had got it on, but because I had actually *finished* something.

*   *   *

From a TV programme, 'Portrait':

My father wanted me to be a lawyer but I told him I was going into the theatre which is the same job, really – but less dangerous to my fellow men.

Man of the Theatre

The versatility of Peter Ustinov needs no further elaboration, yet it is in the world of the theatre that, for me, at least, the name 'Ustinov' strikes the most resounding chord. Yet his father was by no means happy when his son turned to the theatre as a career:

I was a constant source of disappointment to my father. When I managed to pass an audition at the Players' club, giving a turn as the Bishop of Limpopo, my father said: 'Not even drama – *vaudeville!*'

*　　*　　*

Ustinov thinks:

The arts are one of the few known antidotes to the pallor of accuracy and the frigid exhilaration of scientific techniques.

I shall always write as I think, even if I have to boo the gallery from the stage.

*　　*　　*

His friend Peter Jones, who acted with Ustinov in earlier days

and then collaborated with him on a hugely successful radio series,
In All Directions, recalls people commiserating with Ustinov
on the bleak notices for his play No Sign Of The Dove.
Ustinov remarked:

Yes, I had to fight like a stag to get the critics to attack me.

*   *   *

Once theatre stars were chosen just to be themselves. Ustinov
recalls, as a young actor with a walk-on part, being asked by the
star: 'What do you propose doing in this scene, young man?'
Cautiously he replied: 'More or less nothing, I suppose.' At
which the star thundered:

No! I'm the star. In this scene *I* do nothing.

*   *   *

Ustinov made his stage début in a school play in which he was
cast not only as a girl, but as a siren. He was decked out in long
golden curls as one of the nymphs luring Ulysses on to the shoals.
He comments:

Seeing that I was one of the unlikely sirens, Ulysses
rightly wasn't tempted. Instead, he sailed home.

*   *   *

Denis Carey directed Peter Ustinov's Romanoff and Juliet.
Carey remembers that, obviously as a matter of deep principle,

Ustinov was invariably late for rehearsal. Carey remonstrated with him and he was always utterly charming. One day he arrived ten minutes early, having mistaken the call by half an hour. Ustinov disarmed Carey with the remark:

I'm sorry, Denis. Utterly unforgiveable. I assure you such a careless mistake will never happen again.

It didn't, sighs Carey.

* * *

Actor-manager Alec Clunes and Ustinov were discussing the rash of glossy, star-studded revivals that have recently cropped up in the theatre. Ustinov remarked indulgently:

They're all suffering from veneer disease.

* * *

Ustinov admits:

I love hiding behind a false nose. When I stand up as Ustinov to address an audience I feel naked, but I feel absolutely secure behind a disguise.

I like only destructive critics, because they force me to be on my guard and readjust my ideas. To my mind, constructive critics are just impertinent.

* * *

I have a dread of people who say the theatre is their life. They end up in a home where they can't relax comfortably, and where they are expecting the curtain to go up any moment, and they have forgotten their lines.

*   *   *

Ustinov confided to Alan Fairclough of the Daily Mirror:

I will not hide the fact that the fun of having a play on is getting the box-office figures brought to me every night.

*   *   *

When pressed with the unanswerable question Peter Ustinov invariably gives the tongue-in-the-cheek reply:

I went into the theatre because I could not do anything else.

*   *   *

One of his recent plays, described by the author as a 'farcical morality play', but billed as 'a hilarious comedy' outside the Queen's Theatre, is Halfway Up The Tree. *With Robert Morley as its star it was clear that the play would undergo some re-writing as playwright Morley got into his inimitable stride. When Ustinov saw it on tour he merely remarked to Morley and the cast that he thought 'it was very funny':*

MORLEY: That's a relief, Peter. By this time I'm not usually talking to the author.

USTINOV: What? Not even talking to yourself?

Later Jimmy Edwards replaced Morley in the role. Peter remarked to his agent, John Hunter:

I think Jimmy Edwards will be great. My only concern is what he will do to Bob Morley's script.

* * *

Ustinov's play No Sign Of The Dove *had a terrible first-night mauling from press and public. On the second night the author sat in the box and made a brief speech to the audience:*

Thank you very much, ladies and gentlemen. Please don't make me feel too much like President Abraham Lincoln!

* * *

He is not highly in favour of long runs in the theatre for an actor. He confessed:

After eight hundred performances of *Love of Four Colonels* I had become a zombie. I'd say things like 'I'm going now' and wonder what the words meant.

* * *

In his play, Photo Finish, *the leading man appears at four different ages. Ustinov declined at first to play one of the four acting roles, with the excuse:*

It would be impossible to find three other actors who looked remotely like me at *any* age.

* * *

21

Peter Ustinov thinks that acting is undoubtedly easier than writing:

To act well is, of course, difficult. But it is more difficult to write a bad play than to give a bad performance.

*   *   *

Moira Lister was one of the stars of The Love of Four Colonels. *'When it opened at Birmingham,' she recalls, 'it ran for about four hours. Though the audience cheered, the management told Ustinov that he'd have to cut about ninety minutes from his play':*

Why? *Hamlet* ran for four hours – and this play's much funnier.

*   *   *

The nameplate on the star dressing room door at Chichester Festival Theatre *carried the names:* SIR JOHN CLEMENTS, SIR ALEC GUINNESS, MR PETER USTINOV. *On the last night of his play, Ustinov made a speech, saying:*

Of course, we had an uphill battle getting my play on. I mean to say, we didn't have a single knight in it. If anyone wants to know what I'm doing next I'm planning to sail a yacht single-handed round the world.

*   *   *

Actor David Nettheim recalls that Peter was not too pleased when

*car owners were asked not to park in the open area about the
Festival Theatre stage-door. Clements' car alone was privileged
and, without a word, Peter moved his green Maserati. But his
telegram, when John Clements was knighted, read:*

Congratulations, Sir John. Now I see why you need a
whole car park.

*   *   *

When The Unknown Soldier and His Wife *was being
rehearsed, one speech was too long. The actor diffidently said:
'What shall we do about this, Peter?' With mock indifference
the playwright answered:*

Oh, cut it. With luck I won't notice it.

*   *   *

According to Ustinov:

Comedy is simply a funny way of being serious.

One of the most ironic comedies of all is that great
comedians are not comic in real life.

*   *   *

Ustinov told Ann Leslie, then of the Daily Express:

A sudden fit of integrity has seized the acting profession.

It creates a complex among so many established stars who have been hired at vast sums to be themselves but who feel they must justify their fees by becoming someone else.

* * *

On booing in the theatre:

The house-lights should immediately be trained on hecklers. Like owls they cannot hoot comfortably when illuminated.

As witless cries reach you on the stage the first thing to remember is that you are being initiated into the magnificent company of men who have gone through it in the past and have survived with grace and humour.

Novelists are better off than playwrights. You can't boo a bad book. Or if you do you run the risk of being regarded as eccentric.

It is strange, incidentally, that Britain, a country with such a tradition of understatement, should be among the last to dispense with 'the bird' as a form of criticism.

* * *

On glamour:

Glamour in the theatre usually means twenty chorus girls

in a line all doing the same thing like a piece of machinery. It is assumed that twenty women are more glamorous than one.

*   *   *

On Bernard Shaw:

All the characters that GBS disliked had very strong arguments.

*   *   *

Both actors and producers agree that Peter Ustinov is highly amenable to necessary changes being made in his plays, but that he does not care for liberties being taken. He insists:

If there is one word *wrong* in a play of mine I flinch when I hear it. I can sense at once when something on the stage is not right. My nose twitches like a dog's.

*   *   *

On acting:

As an actor, I stretch the possibilities of an audience to its limit.

If you haven't complete *rapport* with the actress with whom you are acting it is like being thrust into the middle of a particularly edgy bullfight.

*   *   *

Agent Eric Goodhead recalls a time when Peter, then aged twenty-nine, was fretting over some theatrical issue with Peter Brook, at that time twenty-five. Ustinov broke the tension by smiling and saying:

The trouble with you, young Brook, is that you're worried about the younger generation catching you up!

*   *   *

Professional to the fingertips, Ustinov was not amused when Danny Kaye pulled out of the Chichester Festival Theatre *season to visit the troops after the Israel–Arab war. He said, slightly sarcastically, to James Thomas of the* Daily Express:

If the war breaks out again and things are not going well for me I can always pull out on the grounds that I must get back and help them out at Amman.

*   *   *

Ursula Jeans and Roger Livesey were having a drink with Peter in Glasgow after a try-out of The Banbury Nose. *Miss Jeans told him that James Bridie had been disappointed in the play but regarded Ustinov as 'our most promising young dramatist'. Ustinov replied cordially:*

How very interesting. I've certainly *always* regarded him as the most promising of our older ones.

*   *   *

Ustinov retains nearly everything he writes in the belief that it may eventually come in useful:

It's wise not to lose one's first draft of a play. On the other hand, it's unwise to cling to it so assiduously that you overwork it with glibness.

*   *   *

Ustinov opinions:

Putting on a play for the public is like opening the door to find a fierce dog behind it. But it's the public that is the dog you have to beware of.

Most of the greatest playwrights have also been actors – Molière, Shakespeare, for instance. They know an actor's problems, even though few of them have been good actors.

I believe that the theatre is a place where anything is permissible so long as the audience, in the main, is kept awake.

*   *   *

Invited to lecture on 'Acting And Its Effect on Playwrights', Ustinov began:

My interest in this subject is entirely passionate and

therefore biassed and therefore unreliable.

*   *   *

Though an admirer of William Shakespeare, his attitude is far from sycophantic. He says:

Shakespeare's hideous stage clowns were the maggots in his apple. Their tortuous banter has become a stress on the ingenuity of producers and a test for the actor's panache. For it requires panache to be gay for a whole scene for no clear reason, with the additional strain of having to pretend to yourself that you know what you're talking about.

*   *   *

His attitude to Catherine the Great as a playwright was also less than flattering:

She once wrote a curious dramatic chronicle in which the characters addressed each other at colossal length in French. The reading of the play becomes rapidly as tedious as those sections of the Bible in which the prophet traces the pedigree of the Israelite Kings back to Methuselah and beyond.

*   *   *

On knowing one's lines:

There is a deep-rooted conviction in the profession that a good text is one that is easy to learn. I don't believe it. I think that in common with most good things a good text is one that is difficult to learn, but even more difficult to forget.

*   *   *

Talking of past successes and failures Ustinov told Geoffrey Willans:

My second play, *Blow Your Own Trumpet*, was well and truly lacerated by the press – but not the public. They weren't there.

*   *   *

Commenting on avant-garde *playwrights and actors he says:*

The *avant-garde* are rushing up a cul-de-sac and by the time they get back to the main road everyone will have gone past them.

*   *   *

Ursula Jeans recalls her and her husband having a drink in a pub with Peter after the word rehearsal at Wyndham's *of one of his plays on opening night. Roger Livesey broke the 'butterflies-in-the-stomach' silence with determined* bonhomie. *He said: 'Well, old boy, they tell me that all you need is a plot of land somewhere and you can go away and forget the whole thing.' Peter replied gloomily:*

All they ever tell me is that what I need is a plot of substance in my play.

Ustinov rarely tries to write an acting role for himself in one of his own plays – though it occasionally happens:

I don't like to foster the idea of Actor Ustinov coming in to save a fragile bauble – a script by Writer Ustinov.

The Write Way

Ustinov asserts:

I act for a living. I write because I must.

I don't believe you can be an angry writer. Anger gets in the way of the plot, and you are no longer creating real characters. You must never forget that you have to be the Devil's Advocate as well.

Too many authors are like fish or birds that want to swim or fly in one direction, change course at the same time and behave alike at the same seasons.

* * *

Johnny Carson, on his New York guest show, asked Peter Ustinov whether he wrote in longhand or on a typewriter. Peter quizzically replied:

I use a quill pen, and my handwriting is meticulous. In fact, all I need is to find a monk who can illuminate the initial letter.

* * *

A reporter asked Ustinov to describe his future writing plans and was told:

I hope to write more serious comedies and funnier tragedies than before.

*   *   *

Ustinovalia:

Shakespeare was probably frowned on by upright people of the sixteenth century as a farmer with the uncontrollable vice of writing. 'Most unfortunate,' they no doubt said, 'he'll give Stratford a bad name.'

The first copy of a finished play is rather like a pair of new shoes. They – and it – will look scruffy in ten minutes.

All writers have a maternal instinct. They cherish the weakest of their creations.

I believe it is a form of decadence merely to be shocking. Shock works on the nerves and not on the intellect and any idea which has to rely on pulling at the nervous system is decadent.

I have very tidy handwriting, but unfortunately it's not

very legible. I like tidy writing. It's like a Bugatti – if the engine looks clean it will work. If a page looks clean it will usually read well.

If I were not a writer I would like to be an international administrator in United Nations, for, as in writing, the whole range of drama, comedy and tragedy is the material at hand.

I must have music when I'm writing. It is probably because I started my writing career during the war and thus had to concentrate to a background of noise from bombing. Now I find silence unbearable and must have radio or even television on all the time. Occasionally I look up and see Bette Davis taking poison but it doesn't distract me.

To someone who is concentrating hard on writing a play there is really no difference between the telephone and a bomb, except that the bomb you can't answer. So that, really, unless it's a direct hit, I prefer bombs to the telephone as music to write by.

The ideal playwright would, like a dog who buries a bone, leave it for a time and, when he has a free moment, from time to time, dig it up. I, too, need to be miserly with my ideas to store and rake them over.

I cannot contemplate the relentless dedication of someone like Lope de Vega who wrote upward of 1,800 plays. I have the faculty of being able to switch my mind on and off.

The business of a dramatist is to ask questions – not to answer them.

English is fine for not saying what you actually mean. French is precise, whereas English is the language of get-out clauses.

I'd rather be regarded as a modern Aristophanes – I haven't been reduced to bringing on people with no pants, but I expect *I'll* be reduced to that.

If you are well known, first-hand research is difficult. If you want to write a Simenon-style thriller about a brothel in Hamburg you can't go into the brothel without people asking you for your autograph.

As a playwright I've learned when to start a play. I used to see the windmill and tilted straight at it. Now I wonder if it is really there; if it's a trap or whether it's worth attacking. Above all, whether it isn't an impertinence to attack it – and, if it *is*, well, what the hell, so much the better – !

*   *   *

Ustinov has frequently been compared with Brecht. This horrifies him:

I admit that, like Wagner, he is a great man: but I can't stand him at any cost.

* * *

To Felix Barker in the Chichester Festival Theatre *programme:*

My method of writing plays can be summed up as the slow approach, the quick thrust, the retreat and the return oblique.

* * *

From Peter Ustinov *by Geoffrey Willans:*

Long words in most languages all sound very similar.

* * *

Stella in Ustinov's play Photo Finish*:*

Books? I don't know what you see in them. I can understand people *reading* them, but I can't for the life of me see why people have to *write* them. When you've read one, you've read them all, I always say.

* * *

Peter Ustinov assured French magazine writer, F Galle, that:

Writing is tough; what is most difficult is to know when to stop.

English is a language I can knock about. I have too much regard for French to do such a thing with it. In English, as in German for that matter, one can say ten thousand things which have no exact meaning, whereas in French each word has its limits.

*   *   *

About the theatre, Ustinov claims that:

Life is far too short to play in long runs.

Pondering Politics

From The Man in The Moon:

Any student of politics will recognise the fact that it is more important to make the right noise than to talk sense.

He was a man of science often selected by the British Government for official missions, since he had a quality of aloof and calculating majesty and an enigmatic quality completed by his utter silence when it was his turn to make a statement.

*   *   *

Peter Ustinov has every sympathy for those who are willing to rebel in what they consider a good cause. But he drily explains his personal attitude thus:

I am a conformist. I am too detached, too Oriental, to be a revolutionary. Calling me revolutionary is like expecting passion from U Thant.

*   *   *

Variety *reported him, when he spoke at a political meeting in Paris, as saying:*

It's much tougher to be an actor than a politician. There are any number of actors who turned to public office, but I can't think of any government official who quit to go on the stage.

*   *   *

His play Romanoff *and* Juliet *had a distinctly political slant and here are some Ustinovisms from it:*

A diplomat these days is nothing but a headwaiter who is allowed to sit down occasionally.

A certain amount of *Das Kapital* was conceived in the British Museum, which makes it all the more remarkable.

Said by a Soviet diplomat in the play:

In the old days it was criminal to believe. With the advent of democracy, we are now given the choice of belief or disbelief, but naturally we are put on our honour to make the right choice. Otherwise, democracy would have no meaning.

A girl in Romanoff *and* Juliet *is with her young lover and is annoyed at a passing soldier. 'Please leave us alone,' she begs him. The soldier replies:*

This is a free country, madam. We have a right to share your privacy in a public place.

Many centuries in close proximity to homesick and miserable soldiers has brought quick maturity to our men and babies of all colours to our women.

US Ambassador (to his wife):

Our daughter has fallen in love with a Communist – and when I say Communist I don't mean a guy who sent a food package to the wrong side in Spain.

These days you have to be very, very strong to allow yourself the luxury of being weak.

Also in Romanoff *and* Juliet *Ustinov wittily satirised the cynicism of the invasion of small powers by the strong and, in describing the history of the mythical country in which it was set:*

If you can find us on the map you will see that our position geographically, militarily, financially, politically, administratively, economically, agriculturally and horticulturally, is quite hopeless. Consequently we have acted as a magnet to the invader throughout our long, troubled history.

The English have been here on several occasions on the pretext that we were unfit to govern ourselves. They were invariably followed by the French on the grounds that we were unfit to be governed by the English.

The Dutch made us Protestants for a while, the Turks made us Mahommedans, the Italians – made us sing quite beautifully.

*   *   *

From Ustinov's play The Unknown Soldier and His Wife:

The saddest profession in the world – an ageing revolutionary.

Even Christ's miracles were political. What convinced the multitude was not a sentiment of love, but the fact that there was suddenly enough loaves and fishes to go round.

*   *   *

Ustinov does not think a great deal of the political parties in Britain. In an article in Atlantic Monthly, *he wrote:*

The Conservatives of today would have horrified Disraeli, while the Socialists would have appalled the Fabians.

In the United States the left wing of one party is much

closer to the left wing of the other than either left wing is to its own right wing.

*　　　*　　　*

Ustinov believes in Trade Unionism. He once said, patting a capacious waistcoat:

I'm an ardent Trade Unionist. I carry sixteen fully paid-up Union cards. This isn't all fat, you know. I should really always be on strike somewhere in this world.

*　　　*　　　*

He defines NATO *as:*

Six nations in search of an enemy.

Like a dinosaur. A tiny brain and an enormous body.

*　　　*　　　*

Says Ustinov:

I once thought of a prayer for a Western European child. He ought to thank God every night for the Americans who protected his liberty. Thank God for the French who are doing what the English ought to be doing and thank God for the Chinese and the Russians, without whom America would be the only country of that size.

He adds wryly:

I told that to an Ambassador at NATO, and he said: 'That's not a prayer for a child – that's a prayer for a NATO Ambassador.'

* * *

Someone asked him if he was a Hawk or a Dove and he replied:

Frankly, I don't care for these aviarists' terms. They tend to be misleading. There's nothing more dangerous than an aggressive dove and very little more ludicrous than a timid hawk. I'd prefer to be seen as an owl, wise, profound and unflappable.

* * *

On ex-President Johnson and American politics:

I once wrote a short story which wasn't published because of the accusation of hitting President Johnson below the belt. It's hardly my fault if LBJ wears his belt like a crown.

President Johnson, in attempting to smooth ruffled feathers, a process in which the hard school of politics has made him an expert, most graciously read out his favourite lines from Robert Lowell's works – lines which turned out to be by Matthew Arnold.

The word 'smear' was, politically speaking, fathered by that eminent parent of the gold-plated phrase, Senator McCarthy, in order to show what the vast army of huge subversive Davids were supposed to be doing to the poor, small fearless Goliaths from Wisconsin.

*　　*　　*

Ustinov frequently refers to the way politicians are using television to put over their image – not always with much success:

Way back, in the Californian senatorial race, George Murphy mumbled and bumbled while Pierre Salinger answered with crystalline dexterity. We all know who got in. The actor disguised as a common man defeated the common man disguised as an actor on a technical knock-out.

*　　*　　*

In 1965, criticising Senator Goldwater, Ustinov neatly summed up his opinion:

The main difference between the Chinese Communists and Senator Goldwater often appears to be that whereas the one have a militant nostalgia for the spirit of 1917, the other has a militant nostalgia for the spirit of 1817.

*　　*　　*

Ustinov remarks that:

43

When a man has too many faculties, he ends up qualifying as a translator with the United Nations.

It requires a slavish devotion to free institutions to allow yourself to be blown sky-high by your protector in the interests of democracy.

*   *   *

On madness in high places:

A thousand years ago the courtiers would know that the king or ruler had gone mad imperceptibly. Today they just wouldn't notice.

Ustinov enlarged on this theme in a lecture:

There is a whole spate of films, adapted from a similar spate of best-selling novels, in which the President of the United States either goes imperceptibly mad, so that nobody notices it until it's too late, or else he's the victim of a sinister military plot by fanatical officers, or else he's powerless to stop the sudden lunacy of an officer with access to a lethal button. No one could call this tendency reassuring, whatever their political outlook.

*   *   *

On Edward Heath, the music-loving Leader of the Tory Party:

Perhaps if Edward Heath had not taken the easy way of politics he might be spending this afternoon recording Beethoven's Emperor Concerto for HMV.

*   *   *

He once referred to Andrew Faulds, the actor turned MP, with the dismissive remark:

A talented actor from the Stratford-upon-Avon company is now giving his performance daily in the House of Commons, in what threatens to be his longest run.

*   *   *

On Liberals:

In America a Liberal is a kind of embryonic 'Commie', a nuisance who asks subversive and embarrassing questions.

The main weakness of the Liberals in Britain is that their platform is occupied by both other parties.

*   *   *

Lecturing at the 1965 Institute of Directors' Conference, Ustinov asserted:

I am one of Liberal convictions and liberal doubts.

*   *   *

45

On political parties:

Great Britain is a Parliamentary democracy represented by three parties of the Centre.

Perhaps, instead of Left and Right, one should refer to the extremes of coeval opinion as Petrified and Flexible.

*   *   *

On foreign affairs:

The Foreign Minister isn't able to replace the clown, but almost everybody is able to replace a Foreign Minister. An FM would be unmasked in a matter of minutes, whereas a clown could probably last for six months before someone said: 'Have you noticed how remarkably intelligent our foreign policy has been lately?'

In the Foreign Office I visualise a small room where people are taught to stutter.

Under the aegis of General de Gaulle France appears to be becoming the last of the French Colonies.

*   *   *

On Harold Wilson:

A Maigret who has the solution but doesn't yet know the crime.

* * *

In October 1968, Peter Ustinov was installed for three years as Rector of Dundee University. In his Installation Address he spoke on politics and student power:

The difference between an ordinary democracy and a people's democracy is that in a people's democracy opinion cannot be freely expressed and therefore goes unheeded, whereas in an ordinary democracy like those in the West, opinion can be freely expressed and therefore goes unheeded.

As a Polish diplomat cynically and accurately said: 'In a capitalist society some people are exploited by other people – in a communist society it is just the other way round.'

In the case of the American Presidency it is the machine which drives the driver and the driver is only required to make reassuring gestures of being in charge of the machine.

The so-called battle for democracy rages in Vietnam in the form of a limited war, a nauseous piece of sophistication. How unlucky it must sound to lose a loved one in a 'limited' war. It is like losing one to a 'clean' bomb.

The giant nations wish to be understood, but more than that, they wish to be loved, and if they're not loved, they'll crush you by God, because they're big and lovable and misunderstood. The Chinese, with eight hundred million souls, are so big, and so lovable, and so misunderstood, they feel they can afford to be hated for a change.

Nearly every political choice these days is a compromise solution. In the effort to appeal to the widest possible cross-section of any given electorate, a colourless candidate is the only safe choice.

When the history of our time is examined by scholars in the distant future, and the centuries shrink to size, Livingstone and Mungo Park will be remembered as the men who opened up Africa with Conrad Hilton not far behind. There may even be some doubt as to which of the three came first.

'Student' is now a label which seems to describe anybody rowdy enough, belonging to a certain age group, just as a great Sunday paper has the endearing habit of describing any low character who peers through boudoir windows or reveals himself in all his natural loveliness to passers-by, as 'a company director'.

The young are on the point of inventing a new language –

or of rediscovering an old one – for an old language spoken with the voice of rediscovery is a new one.

Let us remember that student power, like Government power, black power, white power, flower power, any power, is a trap which sets a period for itself by its very existence.

Power is always superseded by other power: mutual respect is eternal.

And affirming his belief in Youth, the Rector said:

It is youth which has rediscovered love as a weapon. It is youth which has endorsed biblical simplicity in the face of police and police dogs while the odd bishop still blesses arms and fighter-planes.

What makes the ideal leader these days? Rector Ustinov, sadly and cynically answers his own question:

Find a man who will not antagonise the Catholics, Protestants, Jews, Arabs, Buddhists, Agnostics, Negroes, Segregationists, Fascists, Communists, Perverts and Hippies and any computer will tell you that there's your winner.

*　　*　　*

Ustinov suggests modestly:

I was probably picked as Rector of Dundee University because I hover comfortably between the complacently elderly and the eagerness of stretching, student youth.

Or perhaps because:

I had never been to Dundee before. That's probably why they chose me to be Rector of their University.

Films and Filming

Ustinov has won two 'Oscars' and two 'Emmies', and a 'Grammy'. He says:

My awards make very good paperweights. The 'Oscars' are emasculated male figures. The 'Emmies' are, so to speak, emasculated female figures. Between them they should enjoy some excellent mixed doubles at tennis – with 'Grammy' sitting, lonely, umpiring.

*　　*　　*

Sophia Loren was playing an eighty-two-year-old woman in Lady L, a film which Peter Ustinov directed. She inadvertently pulled off a piece of the rubber mask she wore to age her. Peter slapped her hand:

I told you not to open it till Christmas.

*　　*　　*

This film (Lady L) was set in a Parisian brothel. A visiting journalist remarked that he thought the film was a comedy. Ustinov gravely replied:

It's a very wholesome comedy. This is a brothel to which you could take the whole family.

*   *   *

When Walt Disney made nothing but cartoon films Ustinov thought he was the happiest producer in pictures. No problems:

If one of his characters became difficult all he had to do was to erase it.

*   *   *

As a writer, Ustinov is wary of epics:

The Cecil B De Mille type of film doesn't really need a writer. What kind of dialogue are you going to give to the Israelites as they cross the Red Sea? 'Mind that next wave – I don't think it looks steady'?

In a film epic the great thoughts of great men can be whittled skilfully down to a size where they may safely and painlessly go into one ear and out the other, and never detract from the swordplay for a moment.

*   *   *

Filming Spartacus *weighed heavily on him. He says:*

Spartacus wasn't an assignment. It was a career. I was

horrified it would never end. My youngest daughter, Andrea, was born when I started filming it. But by the time I'd finished she was asking my wife where I'd been.

* * *

After filming Spartacus *Ustinov insisted that he would never again wear a toga, or its equivalent:*

To handle a toga properly you have to watch a woman very carefully and notice how she walks and sits down. This type of attention can be grievously misunderstood.

* * *

Another comment on Spartacus *was equally scathing:*

Spartacus must be the first film about an historical subject that took longer to make than the event it was about.

* * *

To a friend he described the film The Egyptian *as:*

A giant speculation about Cecil B Pre-De Mille Egypt.

* * *

He found that appearing in The Egyptian *was somewhat akin to appearing in* Spartacus:

53

Being in *The Egyptian* was like being an extra in an eternal performance of *Aida,* of which the music has been lost.

* * *

Of his costume in The Egyptian *he said it made him look like a Neo-Byzantine prophet:*

But once decided on by Wardrobe it could not be altered. It would need too many front-office decisions.

* * *

For his role in Topkapi *Peter won 'The Supporting Actor' 'Oscar'. It was a comedy thriller based on a museum robbery:*

I don't really know what I was supporting, unless it was the actual museum. I think I really won it for the Best Fat Actor of the Year.

I enjoyed my role in *Topkapi.* I like playing men who aim low and yet miss.

* * *

Ustinov does not entirely approve of film publicity stunts but says that they are not always as useless as they may seem:

When they showed *Cleopatra* in Paris they rented the

entire Underground to bring the guests to the theatre in evening dress. I arrived by car and, for the first time in Paris, found ample parking space.

*   *   *

Peter Ustinov made a French film, Lola Montez, *with Martine Carol, which was directed by Max Ophuls. In a talk at the* National Film Theatre *he nutshelled Ophuls thus:*

He was a man fascinated by both spectacle and the most minute detail and could deal with invisible things on an industrial basis. Max was the type who might make the most beautiful, meticulous and smallest Swiss wristwatch and then hang it on a cathedral for passers-by to see the time.

*   *   *

Ustinov had an early clash with the gentle but firm temperament of Fred Zinnemann, who was directing The Sundowners:

'You can't concentrate with a cigarette in your mouth,' *said the director to the actor.*
'You mean *you* can't concentrate with a cigarette in my mouth,' *replied Ustinov* and, from that moment, all was well between them.

*   *   *

Actor Robin Bailey was in School for Secrets, *the first film Ustinov directed. Bailey noticed a small dog on the set and jokingly remarked: 'Animals as well in this picture?' Peter replied solemnly:*

Yes, it brings in the *Trader Horn* public.

* * *

Cecil Wilson of the Daily Mail *once asked Peter if there were any subjects that he would particularly like to stage or film. Poker-faced, he replied:*

Yes, *Porgy and Bess* on choc-ice and *Nanook of the North* on sand.

* * *

Walter Goetz remembers an occasion at a Cannes Film Festival when Peter deflated an avant-garde *film critic, known for his idolatry of director Jean-Luc Godard. Peter found the long-haired scribe sitting in lonely meditation on the beach and remarked to him:*

Waiting For Godard, no doubt?

* * *

In an interview with Robin Bean of Films *and* Filming *he wittily disposed of pompous film producers:*

Most producers tend to read things before they decide whether they are going to do them. It's only the very, very important ones who say: 'I'm going to shoot The Phone Book next autumn,' having made the decision in all majesty.

* * *

Commenting on Alfred Hitchcock's alleged remark that actors should be treated like animals, Ustinov mildly told the British Film Institute:

Everybody's opinions are formed by their own talent.

* * *

Asked about one of his favourite films, Billy Budd, *which he also directed, Ustinov admitted:*

I didn't want to play Captain Vere in *Billy Budd* because I don't think I'm straight enough. But it was the only way I could get another name without it costing too much. At least I didn't have to go to myself to ask for embarrassing concessions.

* * *

Type-casting is a great problem in filming, he thinks:

At one time I was so eager to avoid type-casting that I'd try almost any character. I used to get scripts in which they'd say: 'We'd like you to play Mr Absolom.' I'd look it up and it said: 'Mr Absolom is a small, thin, balding, nervous

57

man, who speaks with a strong Welsh accent.' I mean, all the things I can't do in one, so I'd say: 'I think you've sent the wrong script.' And they'd reply: 'Aw, Peter, you can do everything. We've *seen* you do everything.'

*   *   *

Peter is a great admirer of the work of Sir Carol Reed, with whom he learned much about filming. He says of Sir Carol:

There's something conspiratorial about his approval when directing, as though he had been charged with the formation of a new cabinet and wished you to accept the Ministry of Agriculture against your better judgment, with the insinuation that you'll probably get the Foreign Office later if you play ball with him now.

*   *   *

He sums up Mervyn Le Roy with this crack:

On *Quo Vadis* there was a scene where two wrestlers were fighting a death battle, uttering nothing but bloodthirsty grunts and groans. Le Roy surveyed them benignly and then said: 'Fellows, make every word count.'

*   *   *

Le Roy once upbraided an Italian actor in Quo Vadis *who was playing Nero's barber, for blowing on the curling tongs he was using: 'Don't blow on 'em! It's too modern.' Ustinov gently deflated him by saying:*

In what century did the wretched Romans stop eating their minestrone piping hot?

*   *   *

Peter will not tolerate hectoring directors or producers. He says:

If a man shouts, his words no longer matter.

*   *   *

On biblical films:

Virtue wins by a Technicolor knockout in the last reel, but up to that moment, the Devil has been leading handsomely on points.

The lions are well satisfied on their diet of Christians so that there is never that cruelty to animals which may offend the susceptibilities of the upright.

*   *   *

In a lecture that Peter Ustinov delivered in Amsterdam he humorously but shrewdly defended the historical film epic:

Many critics attack historical epics for reasons of taste, believing apparently that Roman taste must have been impeccable. It was, I am sure, no more impeccable than Transatlantic taste today and the lapses must have been similar in tendency. You have only to enter the headquarters of an important bank in New York and stroll, intimidated, among the great columns of Gorgonzola and Rocquefort to feel powerful echoes of the Imperial style.

* * *

While filming Beau Brummell *in England with Stewart Granger, Peter disconcerted the Hollywood studio's front-office by sending a Very Important Executive a cable which read:*

GREETINGS TO MY LOYAL SUBJECTS IN THE COLONIES. USTINOV P, PRINCE OF WALES.

* * *

In a recent film, Hot Millions, *the linguistic Ustinov asked that his foreign dialogue be cut down to such basics as 'Oui', 'Si', 'Jawohl', etc. Metro's publicity man, Paul Mills, asked him why:*

I'd rather be an actor than a linguistic stunt-man!

* * *

David Clayton, in the old Illustrated, *reveals how Peter was once hoisted on his own petard through his passion for sending crazy telegrams to film high-ups. He was in Rome, playing Nero in* Quo Vadis. *He persisted in sending cables pointing out historical errors in the script and all signed 'Nero Ustinov'.*

Ustinov eventually proved that he, at thirty-two, was playing a man who had died when he was thirty. He was delighted to get back this cable:

TO EMPEROR NERO USTINOV, ROME. HISTORIC RESEARCH PROVES THAT YOU REALLY ARE DEAD. IN VIEW OF THIS SAD DECEASE WE WOULD BE OBLIGED IF YOUR IMPERIAL MAJESTY WOULD REFRAIN FROM REWRITING THE SCRIPT.

*   *   *

Ustinov doesn't care overmuch for being made up in film studios. He once disconcerted a make-up girl by telling her:

Away, wench! You're wasting your time. My face is far beyond the processes of artificial glamour.

He startled another powder-and-paint artist who was intent on flattening his bushy sideburns, by remarking warningly:

Have care! Those are my landing-flaps for when I sit down.

*   *   *

Ustinov's comments are quick-witted and cannot always be pinned down to specific occasions. Here are some 'caught on the wing':

In filming, a beard is a practical thing. You save one hour every morning in make-up and can therefore sleep longer. Counting on an average film, that amounts to about one hundred extra hours of sleep. It is the actor's only bonus over the audience. No film allows an audience to sleep as long as that.

In the inexplicable film world cowardice increases in relation to the amount of money invested.

The trouble with filming is that you don't see the result of what you are filming until twenty-four hours later, in the rushes. In other words, you're really flying blind. You don't quite *know*. You only *suspect*. Otherwise you wouldn't have to say to your friends: 'I've seen the stuff. It looks marvellous!'

Sheer good looks are suspect in the cinema – they always were slightly. Tyrone Power and Louis Jourdan – both very much better actors than they seem to be – they're just too good-looking to make it seem credible. I know one or two actors who are homely enough for it to be assumed that because they look so plain they must be good actors – and they're not.

One dear old lady in New York told me she just adored me in my film *Millie Mudd*. She assured her indifferent husband that I was a dear really, just in a bad mood when I played in the film!

Nothing makes film producers more cautious than money. If they invest an epic amount of money, they want to see a film that is similar to something else.

I don't like ambitious films any more. I don't like the fact that you have five and a half million dollars breathing down your neck the whole time.

Film studios are like night clubs all over the world. Only the streets outside are different.

Movies are awfully like the army. There are in-trays, out-trays, the orders of the day, and the hot brick of responsibility is thrown about with the speed of a football in a professional rugger match.

I find the standard of film acting now is perilously high. I'm thinking of taking up something else.

Have Curiosity! - Will Travel!

Peter Ustinov, emphatic that he is a world citizen, is the born traveller. He has journeyed extensively, watching the peoples and their habits, listening to them, talking to them, pinpointing their virtues and their weaknesses with sharp Ustinovisms.

On Japan:

It is disconcerting to be naked in a Japanese bath and be massaged by a young girl who has picked up a few English phrases, and remarks, as she is walking up and down your spine: 'Changeable weather we're having lately!'

*   *   *

On Russia:

One of the things about Russia worth encouraging is press interviewing. There they submit an English translation of the article about you for your signature and approval and then pay you thirty-seven roubles and fourteen kopecks for it. A minor snag is that you have to spend the money in Russia – and there's a limit to the number of fur hats a man needs.

Concerto No 1 for a wilting conductor – Peter Ustinov makes his debut with the orchestra while rehearsing for the film, *Hot Millions*. While guiding them through Haydn's flute concerto, the comic conductor, exhausted by his antics, collapses on the rostrum to the delight of an hysterical audience. (Syndication International)

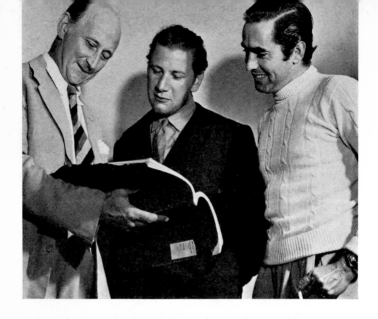

(Above) Sir Felix Aylmer and Tyrone Power look at the script for *Private Angelo* with co-producer and director – 27-year-old Peter Ustinov. (Syndication International) *(Below)* The *Quo Vadis* cast. *From left seated:* Leo Genn; Robert Taylor; Director, Mervyn LeRoy; Producer, Sam Zimbalist; Deborah Kerr; Peter Ustinov *(as Nero)* and Patricia Laffan. *Standing in middle row:* D A Clarke Smith; Nora Swinburne; John Ruddock; Rosalie Crutchley; Finlay Currie; Marina Berti; Felix Aylmer; Elspeth March and Ralph Truman. *In third row from left:* Geoffrey Dunn; Norman Wooland; Arthur Walge; Alfred Varelli; Buddy Baer and Nicholas Hannen. *Seated* is 12-year-old Peter Miles.

Peter Ustinov in the role of father. *Above* with his wife and two-year-old Pavla in 1956 (Syndication International) and *below* with Tamara.

Peter Ustinov as the Archbishop in *The Unknown Soldier and his Wife* at the Chichester Festival Theatre. (John Timbers)

Walt Disney presents *Blackbeard's Ghost* and yet another facet of the versatile Ustinov.

(*Above*) A less serious side of the Archbishop in *The Unknown Soldier and his Wife* (John Timbers) and (*below*) the bewildered Nero in *Quo Vadis*.

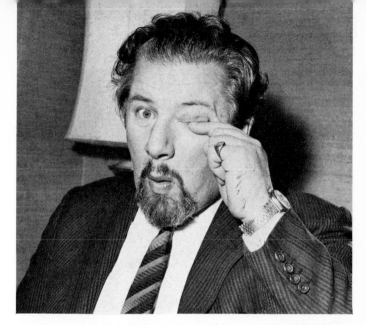

'I have been flying from place to place like a yo-yo for eleven weeks,' exclaims the indefatigable Ustinov who in 1967 had his new play *Halfway Up the Tree* opening simultaneously in London, New York, Paris, Berlin and Dusseldorf. (Syndication International) *(Below)* Taking things a little easier – Ustinov on *The David Frost Show*. (Robert Broeder)

Face to face with Ustinov – sculpture by Enzo Plazzotta (Syndication International) and *(below)* a scene from *Hot Millions* with Maggie Smith.

Russian writing is so square that it becomes octagonal, which is something that those people who use the word 'square' hadn't bargained for.

The Soviet Union is the only corporation in the world larger than General Motors.

In Russia gone are the days when the man guilty of error disappears into the gloom of the Lubianka prison. Now, a board meeting takes place instead, which is perhaps in some respects grimmer.

I sometimes wonder if the Russian revolution really took place at all, and if it wasn't really the anti-trust laws which broke down over there.

*   *   *

In a short story, The Wingless Icarus, *Ustinov wrote:*

For a country which has condemned the cult of personality, Russia is curiously paradoxical. It is practically the only nation which names ships, streets, auto factories and even whole towns after living people. That's why it has to change the names of its streets, ships and cities so often.

*   *   *

From Romanoff and Juliet:

There is no doubt about it. No nation can confess as magnificently or as completely as we Russians do.

* * *

He delightedly recalls his first visit to Moscow where he met an aunt for the first time:

She behaved with absolutely that kind of rather suspect dignity which one got used to in British films during the war. I said who I was and she replied: 'Oh, come in, I've just made some coffee!'

* * *

Ustinov believes that music can be one of the soothing influences in international intrigue:

Even if there is a subversive or reactionary way of playing Beethoven's Violin Concerto, it is frankly beyond the capabilities of the average commissar to detect it.

* * *

Nevertheless he has an ironic suspicion that the powerful Russian nation twigged that music must be treated with care:

Even the glummest of high-ranking comrades recognises a pessimistic symphony when he hears it; the result was that there was a sudden spate of great Russian interpreters playing and pirouetting their way into our hearts and spreading their innocent message of goodwill in all parts of the world.

*   *   *

On Albania:

In Albania inadvertent ironies keep coming out of left field. But to utter is to criticise.

Everywhere are slogans. Anyone who has known penury must feel slightly exasperated that so much energy has gone into this painting and erecting of slogans – especially an inspiring one which read suspiciously like 'Glory To Our Potato Crops'.

*   *   *

Ustinov made a visit to Albania on a conducted tour and is revealing, if slightly guarded, about his impressions:

Never, apart from Haiti, have I sensed people more despised by its own leaders. Albania is Haiti with slogans.

He also noted with interest:

At lunch the table-napkins had dragons painted on them

67

while the toilet paper, rejecting such subtleties, had TOILET
PAPER, MANUFACTURED IN THE PEOPLE'S REPUBLIC OF CHINA
inscribed on the packet.

He found that historical and political data was far from reliable:

One is warned not to ask too many questions and not to
expect too many answers from the questions one does ask.
Our Albanian guide told us that the Castle of Shkodër was
built in the tenth century BC. Since, however, he also said
that the third Five Year Plan had gone into operation as
recently as 1975 we decided to take his statistics with a grain
of salt.

When visiting Shkodër:

A middle-aged Albanian enthusiast said in French:
'Don't stay here – go to Tiranë!' His eyes shot heavenwards
and he blew a kiss. 'Tiranë, c'est comme Paris – the street
lights are on all night!' True enough, but the street lamps
consist of two-watt bulbs hanging by string every four
hundred yards up the street!

*   *   *

*One of his most engaging visits was to a local museum, where
he saw many things which might have been funny but for the
context of his visit. It is characteristic of impoverished and
militant countries that they become fiercely possessive about*

everything which touches them even remotely:

Our birds, *our* bees, *our* flies, the museum guide will insist. In Albania's museum is a large case with a couple of very ordinary-looking stuffed ducks in it. *Our* ducks, we are told. Another showcase is filled with bits of wire and old fuses. The products of *our* heavy industry.

In the section of the museum devoted to recent history there are so many photographs of patriots that one is led to the irreverent conclusion that it is sufficient to help an old comrade across the road to qualify as a hero.

Every face in every picture has the staring look which all Balkan museums specialise in. The patriots all appear to have been caught at the moment of being hanged, even if they died in their beds of old age.

The heads in these Balkan reproductions invariably meet the necks in the wrong places, whereas the tidiest moustache manages to look like a nose-bleed.

The *pièce de résistance* in the museum is a bloodstained shirt 'belonging to a twelve-year-old comrade who was caught and tortured to death by the Yugoslavs'. Never, *adds Ustinov bleakly*, has the good-neighbour policy been pursued with such elegance.

*   *   *

As always, Ustinov saw the odd side of his trip to Albania, as he comments:

Every effort was made to hustle us out of town by 4.15 pm. The shops open again just after that and it is obviously essential to rid the place of foreign bandits before they discover there is nothing to buy.

*   *   *

On Switzerland:

The Swiss are the only nation where the shopkeepers over-cut each other.

*   *   *

On the Middle East:

Everybody understands Israel. I think that the time has come to say that some of my best friends are Arabs.

*   *   *

On France:

There's nothing older than a young Frenchman. They are all prematurely old in spirit.

If I make a mistake in French everybody knows it. If I make one in English they think it's probably deliberate.

The French and the British are such good enemies that

they can't resist being friends.

An English contract is untranslatable into French if it is unskilful, or, if it is skilful, it is open to two or three translations, all of them accurate and all of them different.

The French are logical even in comedy. They aren't very funny but then they fall back on an area where they say they are witty – which is an area of comedy where nobody need follow you. If you're witty enough you won't raise a smile.

*　　*　　*

He explained to Margaret Pringle of Nova *magazine that:*

Our house in Paris has a sort of Turgenev-Utrillo, flaky-sort of body-hoist – because the previous tenant had a heart condition and was also, luckily, the Paris representative of a large elevator firm.

> (*His wife, Suzanne Cloutier, not prone to mar her husband's affable exaggerations, insists that the elevator is because the house was originally divided into apartments.*)

*　　*　　*

He told Sam White of the Evening Standard:

Paris women are truly elegant. They are not terrified

when they hit thirty.

*   *   *

In Atlantic Monthly, *Ustinov wrote:*

To French ears Dean Acheson sounds like one of those physicians immortalised by Molière, who do not wish the patient to get better.

*   *   *

Some passing comments on America and the American way of life. (Not, in any way, to be necessarily confused with Holly-wood!) Don't get it wrong – Peter Ustinov loves America, but:

In America, through pressure of conformity, there is freedom of choice, but nothing to choose from.

At times the United States are about as elegant as an elephant dancing on its points in their attempt to avoid hurting the sensibilities of smaller nations and allies in the vast expediency which makes up the various Atlantic and Pacific alliances.

Americans have accepted the flickering torch of Victorian thinking from two old rivals, Britain and France. And Victorian thinking coupled to ultra-modern technology is a ghastly mixture.

When people talk of equality in Britain they mean women being equal to men. In America it's different. Most Americans would be happy men if their wives would let them be their equals.

There are two countries in the world where irony doesn't exist, America and Monaco. The first because it is too big, the second because it is too small.

*　　*　　*

Ustinov is concerned about America's tepid attitude towards war and politics:

You can go on a television show there and say: 'President Johnson ought to be hanged, preferably from the Statue of Liberty', and the interviewer will say: 'Well, that's a very interesting point of view, Peeder, come back on the show sometime.' Nobody cares because nobody's really listening.

*　　*　　*

Still concerned with America and its attitude to democracy Ustinov remarked in an address to the Institute of Directors:

Americans believe that freedom was their invention. They have been known to send peace-corps groups to Athens to teach the Greeks the meaning of the word democracy.

*　　*　　*

Ustinov's admiration and respect for the States comes out in this searching remark that he made to reporter Jack Bentley:

I'm depressed about America. It's going through a crisis within itself. It is something like Palestine must have been before Christ appeared, a country of minor prophets. Unfortunately, America is also highly concerned with major profits.

*   *   *

In Romanoff and Juliet *Peter Ustinov joked at America's expense when he made an American matron remark:*

I just adore history. It's so old.

*   *   *

In Geoffrey Willans' biography of Ustinov, the dramatist shrewdly remarks:

American democracy is like that of a rich man who hails the porter at his apartment block. 'Hi, Tom!' (his name's really Jack). 'How are the kids, Tom?' (he has no children). Yet both parties are pleased with this friendly transaction.

*   *   *

Peter was once the Mystery Guest on 'What's My Line' in New York. He asked Bennett Cerf if it was all right to make a certain comment. 'Better not,' replied Cerf cautiously. Ustinov replied, with a tinge of acid:

You know, your country is so free here that I never know what I can say.

*   *   *

Commenting on America's preoccupation with health he notes:

In America most people now have an annual check-up every month.

and

Lunch is usually a melancholy meal because nearly everybody stops eating to watch everybody else's diet.

and

Medicine is largely preventative in the States. If you need a cure it only shows you haven't taken enough vitamin shots, which proves that you're careless and stupid.

*   *   *

Jessie Evans, the actress, tells how she was on tour with Peter Ustinov in Crime and Punishment:

I was about twenty-three at the time, young, eager, would-be sophisticated and one evening at the *North British Hotel* in Edinburgh I came down to the bar for pre-dinner drinks all tarted up with a shiny black dress and an excruciating high hair-do. Peter looked at me for a long moment and then said quietly: 'Darling, it's *perfectly* all right if you *want* to look like an American hostess!'

*   *   *

On American democracy:

In America they interpret American democracy as the inalienable right to sit on your own front-porch in your pyjamas drinking a can of beer and shouting out 'Where else is this possible?'

Which doesn't seem to me to be freedom, really, so much as licence.

*   *   *

On a Johnny Carson television guest show Peter was in lively mood on the topic of America:

Noise is a great problem in the States. There are two or three Southern senators who simply can't sleep unless they hear the noise of a filibuster.

I heard about one man in New York who, when they had a cab strike, got on the subway and tried to give them a credit card.

*   *   *

On Australia:

There's nothing worse than an Australian trying to out-blimp the British.

I once visited a small town in the bush. It had thirty-four nationalities. It was like a frontier town in the Balkans at the end of World War One waiting for the League of Nations to turn up and decide which side of the frontier they were on.

*   *   *

On Britain:

English service may be good and the intention kind; but it so often makes it appear like the offer of something when the matron's back is turned.

Britain suffers from the sort of glorified amateurism which produces the terrifying spectacle of a murder trial judge, when he hears that the accused is charged with the murder of her husband while listening to a jazz record, saying vaguely: 'And what, pray, is jazz?'

The Englishman likes to feel that he can laugh at himself. He only does this, however, to take all the pleasure out of laughing at him.

77

The English sportsman prides himself on being a good loser; by being this, he makes sure his opponents feel guilty for having won.

He was serious when he said to Henry Fairlie:

The English are now in search of the violence they lost in the long reign of Victorianism and the aftermath, but this unfortunately often seems to take the form of petulance and flatulence as well.

*   *   *

Ustinov says that in the course of his travels he has discovered that:

People who know too many languages rarely have much to say in any of them.

To arrive at the truth, the German adds, the Frenchman subtracts, and the Englishman changes the subject.

Central Europeans are resilient. They have had to be so often.

The process of demystification in world travel goes on unrelentingly. The most obscure and inaccessible parts of the world are not only on the map, but have regular air services to the great capitals and Kleenex is available.

Nowadays grinning cannibals give friendly demonstrations of their craft to glinting widows from Kansas City: pot-bellied pygmies will blow poisoned darts for a pittance: white hunters help you to shoot your personalised rhinoceros, and on the Amazon they'll shrink a head in forty-eight hours – ask for further information at the desk of your hotel.

*   *   *

Jokingly, he insists that he is not multi-lingual:

This is a false legend built up by unscrupulous press-agents. I can only speak French, German, Italian, Spanish and Russian – and I can survive in Serbo-Croat; but then I have a great gift for survival.

*   *   *

Peter is notoriously unpunctual and finds the clock an unfeeling enemy:

I'm never on time for an appointment in England or America. In France I'm always on time because everybody else is always late; but in Spain, where nothing starts until midnight, I'm always early.

*   *   *

79

Is he disillusioned with travel? No; yet he wrote in the Sunday Telegraph:

It is not only individuals who think of keeping up with the Jones's. Nations now devote vast stores of energy and develop complexes keeping up with each other, and in order to keep up with the minimum effort, they imitate each other.

*   *   *

He has a boat which is a source of joy to him and he says:

We (the family) try to visit a new country every year in the family ketch *Nitchevo,* anchored at Cannes. My only fear is that we may run out of countries before the children grow up and leave us.

*   *   *

Accustomed as he is to rushing round the world by train, plane and car, Ustinov still notes, shrewdly:

In the past seventy years man's capacity for displacing himself through space has increased to a far greater extent than it ever did from pre-history to 1900. All that has *not* improved perceptibly are man's actions when he arrives at the end of his journey.

Speaking for Others

Says Ustinov: 'Peter Jones and I had met in Crime and Punishment *where, as members of the Czarist Police, we tracked down Sir John Gielgud eight times a week. After a long and faithful term in the service of Little Father a BBC comedy programme was the logical outcome. The result was* In All Directions.'

Adds Jones: 'Peter Ustinov's flair for parodying phrases, styles and ideas is as great as his flair for mimicry and accents. We hit on the idea of parodying sayings and writings that MIGHT have emanated from well-known people. I never ceased to be amazed at both the speed and accuracy with which Peter hit the target. Here are some that I retained':

Don't help every lame dog over a stile – he may be happier where he is.

(*George Bernard Shaw*)

Give me oblivion and you may keep your dreams.

(*Sigmund Freud*)

Love, my dear Aynesworth, is called gallantry in the drawing-room, lust in the bedroom, greed in the pantry, inattention in chapel and an appreciation of nature in Norfolk.

(Oscar Wilde)

To spill a vase is not a sin; it is but sinful to hide the pieces under the bridge.

(Chinese Proverb)

Suffering is the wine which heightens the meal of routine.

(Walt Whitman)

A woman will never sell what she can give away for a profit.

(de La Rochefoucauld)

If you spend your life weeping it is cold comfort to die laughing.

(Sir Charles Dibb)

Ask for the world and you'll get a peanut; ask for a peanut and you'll lose what you've got.

(Rockefeller)

What is the life force of man, sir? Blood, say you? Or water? Or sherry? Or sack? None of these, sir, I say, but ink, sir, ink.

(Dr Johnson)

A chaperone is one too old to tempt, but still young enough to know temptation; a maiden is one too young to tempt, and not old enough to know temptation; thus must the gallant make love to one for the other's favours, and bear the chill of autumn when dressed thinly for the spring.

(Cellini)

A prophet without a message is like a wheel without a cart.

(Confucius)

A decision must mature like port. It's not worth taking until the moment is almost past.

(Wellington)

A moment is what separates success from failure.

(Napoleon)

Laughter by itself is foolish, but laughter at a joke is good.

(Swedenborg)

The lover will call a sparrow a heron; the spouse will call a heron a sparrow; the wise man will call a sparrow a sparrow and stay single.

(Chinese Proverb)

Yes without No is like wine without a glass – unpalatable.

(Tallyrand)

The sound of bat meeting ball, of a dog barking and a pretty woman laughing – give me these and you may keep your symphonies.

(Sir Edward Elgar)

No game can have more than one winner. If you dread losing, don't play the game, but you will then suffer, for not having played, you will never know if you could have won. It is better for the peace of mind not to entertain games in your own household, and never to accept invitations to houses where games might conceivably be played.

(Japanese Proverb)

If you laugh all the time when you don't get your way, if you laugh at misfortunes that happen each day, then you'll probably laugh when they take you away.

(Patience Strong)

Don't look for the 'originals' of these sayings and truisms elsewhere. These skits on the styles and thoughts of the people named were all written by Ustinov, and broadcast by the BBC.

Hollywood – a State of Mind

Peter Ustinov, no fool, is aware of the value of Hollywood to his career and he enjoys much of this legendary showplace and its surroundings. And its people. But with shrewd wit he has penetrated much of its sham and flamboyance:

In Los Angeles one gets a certain nostalgia for England. There are certain mornings when vision is restricted by a deep lifeless smog. Then one can forget all the travel posters and almost cheerfully believe that one is back in Uxbridge or even Slough.

Working with an old-type Hollywood director is rather like going through the Customs – you have to keep explaining what tricks you have in your bag.

Few Hollywood top executives seem sure of their friends, but they all seem absolutely sure of their enemies.

Michael Curtiz was a remarkable Hollywood director, with absolutely no pupils to his eyes at all. He'd forgotten all his Hungarian and hadn't learned any English, so he was permanently stuck in a language limbo. Communication with Curtiz was a piece of linguistic legerdemain.

Hollywood can be exuberantly hospitable. They go 110 per cent of the way to meet you.

Hollywood represents the true democracy of art, in which the ignoramus with the gift of instinct argues it out with the professor crammed with knowledge and rancid ideals.

The Japanese gardener in Hollywood is an underprivileged person. He comes to mow the lawn and trim the hedge in a mere 25 hp Straight-Six Convertible.

In Hollywood they say that there are only two things an actor can't get over – bad women and bad scripts.

Traffic cops sort out the traffic with a magnificent rudeness which makes even the most high-powered executive in his Oldsmobile feel that his journey is more like From Here to Eternity than From Here to Paramount.

In Hollywood the unreal and the real seem to get mixed up so that they tend to set your social status by the role you're playing. In my first film there I played a serf and they almost treat you like a slave. 'Come here!' they shout, brutally. They forget that you are but an actor employed for servile delineation. My second film was *We're No Angels* and it upped my social standard. Instead of playing a slave I was playing a convict. It was important, for a convict, unlike a slave, was a man who was free once. But I had to be careful never to give the impression that at night I was escaping from the studio.

Hollywood is full of men of fifty who look after themselves with such assiduous application that they look like a very healthy sixty.

Only in Hollywood exist grown men who have never thrown off romantic conceptions of the past. History to these dear hearts is a surprising and wonderful dream that has never really been lived.

*   *   *

He is often caustic about the social life in generous Hollywood:

A host in Hollywood is someone who is never quite sure who will turn up.

Cocktail parties in Hollywood are quite a problem. You can go to as many as four in one evening and very likely have been expected at two of them. The only people who you know are likely to be the catering staff. I considered that I had beaten the system when one head waiter whispered to me: 'Where's your coat, Mr Ustinov? I'll put it somewhere handy. I doubt if you'll want to stay here very long.'

Gunplay is no longer practised at Hollywood parties except in melodramatic circumstances, but enmity is cultivated with incredible application and technique.

* * *

Peter summed up the edgy situation in the film metropolis thus:

You can assess a man's position in Hollywood by mentioning his name to a Big Shot tycoon. If he replies, with almost indecent haste: 'Just one hell of a great guy – just the greatest. I sent him a platinum cigarette case on his daughter's wedding', you can be sure that he's talking about someone he can't abide. But if he replies with melancholy: 'Yeah, a great guy, but goes with the wrong people' you can be sure that he does not represent a commercial menace and that consequently a degree of friendship can be allowed to seep into the condolences.

* * *

Terence Stamp will never forget a long road publicity tour he made with Peter Ustinov in the States in connection with Billy Budd:

I was wilting from the same old questions being asked by journalists, film people and the public and I asked Peter: 'How do you keep so fresh?' 'These people fascinate me', Peter replied. 'It's utterly fascinating to see just how long so many people can be so boring in so many ways!'

* * *

From The Man Who Took It Easy:

Walking in Hollywood is tantamount to loitering with intent.

* * *

He has told several reporters (including some in Hollywood) that:

Dictatorship in Hollywood is the best sort of government, provided you are the dictator.

Passing Thoughts on Passing Matters

On optimism and pessimism:

An optimist is one who knows exactly how sad the world can be, while a pessimist is one who finds out anew every morning.

* * *

From The Unknown Soldier and His Wife*:*

An artist can always exercise his curiosity on the grounds of a search for material.

* * *

Ustinov has crowded a lot into his less than fifty accomplished years, yet he's still an advocate of patience:

Take your time. To be in a hurry is to kill your talent. If you wish to reach to the sun it isn't enough to jump impulsively into the air.

* * *

Peter Ustinov, when asked if he had any desire to reach the moon, replied briefly:

No, but I would like most people to leave for it.

*   *   *

On jazz:

This is an art form which probably stems from a spirit of revenge by the negroes for having been taken to America at all.

*   *   *

On fashion:

Modern fashions change so quickly that I have suggested that *Vogue* and *Harper's Bazaar* should become daily papers.

He does not think the modern girl's fashions are deplorable:

The dirtiest periods in history were when most was covered – like the Victorian era. Today, it's all strip and no tease, and that cannot be altogether a bad thing. Then, it was thirty minutes' strip and husband came in.

*   *   *

When Jessie Evans was touring with Peter in Crime *and*

Punishment *she remembers Edith Evans wearing a rather awful and skittish hat. Peter changed carriages and firmly announced:*

I can't bear to sit opposite that jockstrap a moment more!

*   *   *

Peter attended a small lunch arranged by David Lewin, then of the Daily Express, *for an interview-story. He surveyed the bread-sticks which had been carefully placed at crazy angles in glasses by the diligent headwaiter. Ustinov, unimpressed, remarked:*

Ah, I see the tables been decorated by Henry Moore?

*   *   *

On artists:

Franta Belsky, the Czech sculptor, once did a bust of me. He made me look, perhaps rightly, like an omniscient satyr.

*   *   *

For the film Blackbeard's Ghost *artist David Jones was hired to paint a full-length portrait of Ustinov as the genial pirate-ghost. Said Peter jovially:*

It was an extraordinary likeness, but I'd be afraid to hang it in my own house. My dogs would never stop wanting to be fed by it. Or maybe they'd never stop whining.

*   *   *

When sitting for a bronze multi-head by Enzo Piazzotta he proved quite a burden to the artist. He first turned up with a beard, then a moustache and then cleanshaven. Piazzotta exploded, but Peter explained that he was playing an Archbishop in The Unknown Soldier and his Wife, *and melted the artist with the disarming, soft answer:*

Who ever heard of an Archbishop with a 'tache?

* * *

From his short story Man In The Moon:

The world is not run by historians. It is a luxury we cannot afford.

* * *

Ustinov says: 'I'm a great believer in beginner's luck. That's why I try so many things.' Yet this versatile man has been constantly plagued by suggestions that he diversifies his talents too much, instead of canalising them. True? Ustinov wonders. On the Johnny Carson show he said:

I don't do nearly as much as people think. When I've written a play and it's perhaps staged the same week as I publish a book, everyone thinks I've done it all at once, like writing with both hands simultaneously. I don't.

In a lecture to the British Film Institute he said:

Is it dangerous to spread talent? I don't know. But I imagine that Leonardo da Vinci must have been constantly irked by people telling him he ought to concentrate on doing more Mona Lisas instead of messing around with drawings for siege-machinery. Incidentally, I think the Mona Lisa is highly over-rated. She looks like the matron in an inferior hospital, with a sort of mind-over-matter look. Perhaps da Vinci painted her as a target for his siege-machinery?

*   *   *

On physical courage:

People of sedate characters spend their weekends away from the office sky-diving with expressions of almost erotic elation in their faces – expressions which would invite dismissal during the week.

*   *   *

He made a delightful film called Hot Millions, *a satirical comedy about computers. But it is clear that he does not fancy the Computer Age. He finds it significant that:*

A Danish lady of one hundred and four was summoned to enrol in a nursery school the other day, because the computer only went up to ninety-nine, and she appeared on the records as being five years old.

The terrible injuries meted out by an ailing computer

will make the sacrifices of the early saints seem like isolated bits of bad luck. A mad computer is in all probability even more dangerous than a mad man.

God will eventually be eliminated by computers. They will eventually answer questions that haven't even been put.

Some people say computers are better than people – but they don't get much fun out of life.

In this film (Hot Millions), *the theme was also about embezzlement, and Ustinov, who wrote the screenplay with Ira Wallach, justified his embezzling on the grounds that he was insured by the firm against such risks. He argued:*

A midwife needs a baby and an undertaker needs a corpse; and an insurance company needs an occasional embezzler to remind them what they're in business for.

* * *

On patriotism:

Practically every game played internationally today was invented in Britain, and when foreigners became good enough to match or even defeat the British, the British quickly invented a new game.

* * *

On ambition:

My ambitions are impressive, but also mainly secret. However, I admit to one ambition. I would like to make enough money to enable me to afford to live the way I do live.

*   *   *

Producer George Brown remembers Peter staying one night at the 'Bull', Oxford, a hotel noted for its frequent Freemason functions. 'I asked Peter if he had slept well,' says Brown, 'and he replied':

Afraid not. A party raged all night and the hotel reverberated with the sound of falling masonry.

*   *   *

From Halfway Up The Tree:

'You're sure your mother didn't send you abroad because you were committing suicide a little too often?'
'Yes, that's quite true. The neighbours objected.'
'Neighbours *always* object, don't they?'

In this age of mass-communication, folly is contagious.

No man should be alone to face huge horizons. Even in

Noah's Ark there were no bachelors or spinsters among the animals.

*   *   *

From There are 43,200 Seconds In a Day:

He described a lyric soprano as looking like a giraffe. Her neck was so long that you could practically follow the notes on the way from the diaphragm to the open air.

*   *   *

About his boat Nitchevo:

It can sleep six people who know each other very well. Or one prude.

*   *   *

Ustinov once tackled the task of producing an opera:

Opera singers learn to act quickly and soon master all the gestures. Unfortunately, they soon forget everything except the gestures. Not that it matters much, for on the first night they proceed to do exactly what they did in the last opera.

*   *   *

He on one occasion tried to fix a lunch date with the film executive Lord Rank, according to agent Eric Goodhead. Rank kept flicking and re-flicking through his diary and turning down all Ustinov's suggested dates. Eventually, Lord Rank said: 'How about Thursday, the —th' naming a date nearly four weeks ahead. Without hesitation Peter remarked:

So sorry, that is the one date I can't make.

*   *   *

His secretary, Liliane Couturier, says that working for him is a source of enjoyment and fun, but one cannot keep up with his witticisms. She admits that she has forgotten most of his cracks but these she recalls:

I jokingly told him to stop patting his own back. He flashed back: 'It's a long time since I've been able to reach it.'

He once intervened on somebody else's behalf on a certain matter and I made a Gallicism: 'You have a long arm.' He replied: 'No, just a lot of push – due to my weight.'

*   *   *

Incidentally, he once started a campaign on behalf of the virtues of being fat:

'Fat' has become a dirty word and fallen into disrepute. It used to mean 'abounding in riches, well-furnished, well filled out.' Now it just means 'not slim'.

*   *   *

Peter Ustinov's ability to fit in with all shades of society and in all phases of culture and show business is perhaps explained by his remark:

There is no incompatibility between Barnum and Beethoven; both have their place in a cultured society.

* * *

He is an ardent tennis player, as well as a regular at Wimbledon. He explained to the Daily Sketch:

I don't consider my stomach a handicap in tennis. It's a kind of secret weapon. People don't expect people with a paunch like mine to be agile on the courts. It takes them by surprise when I dash, and don't waddle, to the net. I'm used to dealing with my problem on court. If I became thin I would be completely off-balance, and bang would go my secret weapon!

* * *

He describes cricket as:

An irritating game which I loathed mainly on account of the ball being much too hard.

I know that cricket has inspired many great Englishmen: I can't help it that the sound of bat on ball makes my teeth grate.

* * *

He is not very keen on horseback riding either:

Sitting on a horse is one of the most nightmarish experiences I know. I have had this feeling ever since I heard about my great-uncle, who was the General Commanding the Cossacks' 'Savage' Division. He was so heavy that when leading them in a charge he was constantly humiliated by having them pass him before they reached the enemy.

*   *   *

Music is yet another dominating influence on Peter Ustinov:

Someone gave me a baton when I was young. Since then I've conducted practically every big orchestral work – in front of a radiogram.

For *Quo Vadis* I had to learn to sing and I attended the Rome Opera House for lessons. My first appearance was dramatic for it coincided with a particularly poor reception of the company's *Samson and Delilah*. Since I'd grown my hair long to play Nero, the rumour quickly spread that I was a new tenor engaged for the opera. The rumour was quickly dispelled when I started to sing.

The Maestro was frank with me. He said: 'Of course, three lessons is ridiculous. To teach you to sing I need six years.'

After Lesson One he said: 'Try to breathe with your forehead.' After the second, 'Think with your diaphragm.' After the third, 'Whatever you do, do not forget to sing with the eye.'

Had I followed this advice I might at least have made history as the world's most anatomical singer.

*   *   *

From The Man Who Took It Easy, *a short story by Ustinov:*

Basically, Beethoven was a fool. A few more *schottisches* and a few less symphonies, and he could have lived more comfortably, even have gone to the expense of an ear-trumpet, perhaps.

Outside there were trees, grass, water, the same phenomena which had sparked Beethoven in his Boy Scout hike in the hackneyed Sixth and Mendelssohn in his Cook's Tour in the Scottish and Italian symphonies.

Erhardt's sonata for three drums was an immediate success and had the honour to be hissed at the annual meeting of the International Society for Contemporary Music. The news of this fiasco *d'estime* spread far and wide and Erhardt was asked to lecture in America.

*   *   *

From a lecture to the Institute of Directors' Conference in 1965:

Purcell, who died when Bach and Handel were ten years old, was a very great composer, whose importance in

Britain would surely have been recognised earlier had his name been Heinrich Pürzel.

* * *

On talent:

It is not enough for a country to breed talent. It must eventually deserve it.

* * *

Ustinov says:

I'm happier in England than elsewhere but I can't say that *Land of Hope and Glory* brings a lump to my throat – especially when sung by Clara Butt!

* * *

On Wagner:

For me, Mozart's music is the best. Wagner is a soporific. I once went to Munich determined to see *Lohengrin* through. I even went into training for it by going to bed early three nights running. But at the performance I woke to find people stepping over my feet in the interval. I had dropped off during the overture even before the curtain went up.

* * *

In 1968 he accepted a new challenge by producing Mozart's The Magic Flute *in Hamburg. He concentrated on the magic fairytale quality. He remarked gleefully:*

The three boys who delivered the magic flute were supposed to drift through the air in a Montfgolfier balloon. They usually came coasting in on a sort of Baroque mantelpiece.

Theatrically, *The Magic Flute* is an absolute ragbag. The Italians have the right attitude to it. They call it a heroic comedy.

Thinking again of The Magic Flute, *he said:*

I'd like to have brought the lions on for the final curtain, with Union Jacks on their tails, perhaps, and holding up an appeal to devalue the mark.

*   *   *

Some passing thoughts on love, marriage and women:

Demanding emancipation for all women is like insisting that everybody should vote, even if there is no candidate that represents your point of view.

Complete equality between the sexes doesn't work unless tempers are equable – and who ever heard of a woman as even-tempered as a man?

*   *   *

From Romanoff and Juliet, *this cynical crack:*

SHE: Have you known many women?
HE: I am a sailor by profession.
SHE: Thank you for your honesty.

*　　　*　　　*

On bachelors, from Photo Finish:

Our Lord was a bachelor, and it's safe to assume that his instructions were theoretical rather than practical in these matters.

He's a bachelor born. Wears a cloth cap and drives in an open sports car, mainly in wet weather.

And from There are 43,200 Seconds In A Day:

Edward, a bachelor, always blushed at the thought of the process which had given him life, since his parents had always seemed to him far too nice to forget themselves in such an intensely personal way.

*　　　*　　　*

A character in one of his plays remarked to a girl:

You've the mind of a man with all the other attributes of

your own sex. It's an ideal combination.

*　　*　　*

And, of another woman:

She has the shape of a girl who spends a lot of time on a horse. She leans forward as she walks and looks as though she is about to take a fence.

*　　*　　*

When asked what attracted him most about a woman, Ustinov replied, drily:

When a man's attracted to a woman all rules go out of the window.

*　　*　　*

He thinks that women must rebel at the remark:

Well done, you did that just like a man!

*　　*　　*

Ustinov married his second wife just as he had to leave for Hollywood to play a slave. At the wedding reception he cracked:

What impeccable timing for such a decision.

*　　*　　*

Asked by Henry Fairlie whether women had influenced him he remarked:

It's a bit early for stock-taking. But that doesn't mean that I intend to have three more wives.

*   *   *

Ustinov says that:

Watching children grow up is a great delight. You see in them your own faults and your wife's virtues, and that can be a very stabilising influence.

*   *   *

Old Sam in Photo Finish*:*

When you're very old you know that children have the right idea. If only they had the authority.

*   *   *

Also from Photo Finish*:*

SAM: Lady Chough promised us a Pomeranian for a wedding gift.

REG: I can imagine few more useful gifts to a young couple.

*   *   *

Again in his play Photo Finish *Ustinov provided one of the wittiest and off-beat comments on sexiness when a middle-aged man remarked:*

It must be fun having nails done, isn't it? There's something backhandedly sexy about having your fingers held by a scented girl and then letting them dangle afterwards in a lukewarm bath. It's as though each little finger was a roué on its own, with an independent life and independent pleasures.

*　　*　　*

He does not gladly suffer bores or sycophants:

I find that a most effective way of quelling bores is simply to say, suddenly and irrelevantly: 'Now, Singapore – does that mean anything to you?'

*　　*　　*

A friend described how Ustinov once disposed of an obnoxious member of the nouveau riche. *The blowhard, boasting, remarked: 'I had an American steamer-car that burned industrial oil':*

'Really?' *replied Peter,* 'I once had a Spanish steamer-car that burned heretics.'

*　　*　　*

He thinks highly of laughter:

The main difference between man and animal is man's ability to laugh.

We should laugh more often. Everybody wants to win prizes and honours and the way film juries are put together you can't win a prize with a funny film. They enjoy a weak drama more than a strong comedy.

*   *   *

On justice, from There Are 43,200 Seconds In A Day:

This (the Old Bailey) was the place where British justice was dispensed, the place where men were told they were innocent until proved guilty, but where the atmosphere told them that they were pretty guilty even if proved innocent.

The judge, Lord Stobury, had the characteristic traits of his profession. A vulture's head was set below the hunched line of the shoulders, the white wig seemed to be powdered with the dust of death.

*   *   *

On money:

Money corrupts – particularly those who don't have any.

I think of money only when I have none left. My greatest luxury is to forget that it exists.

I never worry about revealing my earnings to the tax-man. Why should he worry? After all, he gets it all.

*　　*　　*

On hippies:

The reason they are like this is because they are trying to find the essential goodness we lost on the way to civilisation.

Don't accuse hippies of idling. They're rebelling – jus-tifiably, I think – against the stupidity of their forerunners. That should keep them very busy.

I'm delighted about hippies in Hollywood and San Francisco. It is somehow beautifully ironic that bare feet should now tread the world's most glamorous sidewalks.

*　　*　　*

On LSD:

It provides the same hallucination that a medieval nun once obtained by starving.

*　　*　　*

From The Indifferent Shepherd:

HUGH: There's nothing to be afraid of, what with all this modern science.

HENRY: I'm afraid of modern science more than anything.

*　　*　　*

Ustinov once remarked to actor Peter Jones:

Clichés are highly horrible things, but truths must be said. In the end you find that all clichés are true – and that's the bitterest pill of all.

*　　*　　*

At a party Peter made a quip and burst into a peal of laughter. He apologised thus:

I don't laugh at my own jokes unless they're very good. That one was particularly good.

*　　*　　*

Ustinov has decided likes and dislikes:

I like to give occasional parties, especially in Paris. Our last one went on to four o'clock in the morning but we had no complaints. Just three letters from total strangers saying how much they'd enjoyed an enchanting evening!

I like press interviews. They force one to crystallise one's flood of thought.

I like dogs. They rarely argue with me.

I do enjoy food, but I cook nightmarishly. The only time I lose weight is when I cook for myself and it is so nauseating that I keep thinking, 'Oh well, I'll wait for the next meal.'

I very much dislike people who pick their teeth with a covering hand.

I hate the thought of resting on my laurels. Laurels can come to feel very much like holly.

Two forms of animal life that I dislike intensely are lip-readers and people who pose a question but can't wait for a reply. I think most of the latter breed become television interviewers.

*　　*　　*

It was self-revealing when Ustinov made a character in Add A Dash Of Pity *remark:*

I'm only killing time, and I find I'm damn bad at it.

*　　*　　*

Also in Add A Dash Of Pity *he makes one character say:*

'You must have some opinions!' said Oxford, who loathed the pomposity of the joyously downtrodden.

* * *

From Word In The World's Ear*:*

He was more tortured, more hesitant, with the face of a St Bernard forced to travel with his cask empty.

* * *

On criticism and critics:

Never make a friend of a critic. They feel guilty if they are a friend of yours and go out of their way to slate you. I've always discovered that when you slight a critic he gives you a good notice.

In all societies criticism is encouraged just as an engineer places safety valves on an engine; there has to be somewhere for the steam of opinion to escape.

Although criticism is encouraged in civilised communities it does not for a moment imply that it should be listened to – or even heard.

* * *

From Romanoff and Juliet:

I began life as a ne'er-do-well but was found cheating at cards, so my career was finished.

* * *

From Photo Finish:

In my day there were things that were done and things that were not – and there was even a way of doing the things that were not done.

* * *

From Moment of Truth:

Modesty is the unhealthiest form of introspection.

* * *

Ustinov has frequently been involved, very warily, in administration and sees the pitfalls:

There's nothing more frustrating than sitting on the board of, say, the Arts Council and present all the façade of allocating inadequate moneys, which, after they've consulted you, the permanent officials do exactly what they like with.

* * *

He will sometimes use the description 'old-fashioned' for a man on the grounds that:

Old-fashioned is the word most calculated to frighten even the most old-fashioned executive.

*　　*　　*

On suburban civilisation:

Suburban civilisation makes grim demands. Caravanners travel miles to set up their tents in accurate rows in camping preserves which supply the comforts of nomadic life from well-stocked kiosks. I can understand the call of the wild: the call of the car-park is a little more esoteric.

*　　*　　*

On official dress:

Why do people dress up for formal occasions? I find the launching of battleships or something like that, an irresistibly comic spectacle. Why do people have to put on hats with feathers blowing in the wind? I see no difference really between that and tribal garb in the African jungle.

*　　*　　*

Perhaps Ustinov was not thinking about the old adage 'Those who live in glass houses', etc, when he made these remarks:

I find it extremely amusing to go into a shower bath after

a game of tennis and see a man with no clothes on but wearing an expression on his face as if he *is* dressed. Sometimes at a place like the RAC you get four generals who have just played squash and their clothes are hung up and they're absolutely purple in the face, with a line round their necks and the rest of them as white as a sheet – and they're looking into the distance and clearing their throats and discussing things as though they were dressed. It's these moments in life which I think are really indicative of the follies and pretensions of human beings.

*　　*　　*

Ustinov, a great car fanatic, once owned an Hispano-Suiza. He said of it, lovingly:

The nice thing about it is that you can drive up alongside a bus, look down at the driver and say 'Good morning.' I must admit I find it a game awfully difficult to tire of.

*　　*　　*

He once had a secretary to try to keep his papers and appointments in order. It was a losing battle. He remarks:

I must have inspired her with my own brilliant disorder, for she got her own back by writing a play which was very, very good.

*　　*　　*

Walter Goetz recalls dining with Peter and some friends in a

H*

very chi-chi Paris restaurant. Some American tourists sent the waiter over for Peter's autograph and then, out of appreciation, sent back a Kennedy silver dollar. Peter said to Goetz that while quite prepared to give his signature he saw no reason why it should be fixed at a dollar a time. From the wife of a film producer he borrowed an Italian 'jeton', a token used in Italy for telephoning. He sent it to the Americans with the following note:

An old Russian proverb, which I have just invented, states that no one may accept a gift unless he can return one of the same value. Please therefore accept this Italian 'jettone' used by Mussolini in *circa* 1943 to ring up Clara Petacci.

*　　*　　*

Goetz once took Peter to a big sale in Paris and a Renoir was up for auction. Peter remarked that he liked this painting of the German artist 'Wiedershwartz', which is a straight German translation of Renoir. That started an endless punning game called re-naturalising the painters. Most of Peter's endless examples require a precise ear for phonetics as well as a knowledge of English, French and German. But among those he sent me in a note were:

Queerwater (for Bouguereau); B. Snackbar (B. Buffet); Gentile (Goya); Oderfeder (Orpen); Dixans (Teniers); Auslander (Forain); Whoknows (Quizet); Pierre Absinthe (Pieter de Hooch); Grandmother (Gromaire).

And he signed it, 'Your servant, P. Genuggebraucht' (which translated comes out as P. Usedenough).

*　　*　　*

Here is a favourite remark of Ustinov's. He has used it, over a longish period, in various countries, on divers occasions – in interviews, speeches, lectures – and in many contexts, applying it, aptly, to tycoons, politicians, actors, writers and members of the Church. I have not risked asking him to enlarge on it.

Very often the people who make it to the top have no qualifications to detain them at the bottom.

*   *   *

Ustinov was once invited to address the Massachusetts State Legislature, where they have some traditions that have been lost in England. As he reached the Legislature Hall the Speaker of the House of Representatives said: 'Halt, who goeth there and dareth ye to enter?' He recalls:

It was a disconcerting welcome and I couldn't decide whether or not he had forgotten I was invited.

*   *   *

The occasion may be forgotten, but the wit remains. Here are some of Ustinov's observations:

To be mild, to be tolerant, to be wise and sensible – you've got to be really tough.

The trouble with the people who live for revenge is that

they're never quite sure when they've had it – and so, to be on the safe side, they go on and on, endlessly.

No one can approach in imbecility the wise man besotted by his own wisdom.

Style is a way of lying. It is an ornament which hides the architecture.

To know one's rights is one thing. To exercise them is another.

The more we are encouraged to express opinions, the fewer opinions we find there are to express. It is indicative that the largest turnout at elections are always where there is only one candidate.

Where there is no choice all men are friends.

Life is imperfect and therefore it must be lived to the full.

The Angry Young Man's 'Damn you, England!' seems to me to be really a form of narcissism.

The tramp is to the beatnik what the workman is to the idle rich. The tramp works hard at not working; the beatnik, just idly, doesn't work.

Beware of experts. The day humans blow up the world with The Bomb the last survivor will be an expert saying it can never happen.

It was Danton in the French Revolution who coined the phrase 'Audacity, audacity – for ever audacity!' This fine sentiment led him to the guillotine. The public prosecutor, Fouquier-Tinville, on the other hand, showed no audacity whatsoever. He clung to a deadly central course in a time of violence. As a consequence he lived a year longer than Danton and also ended on the guillotine. *Moral:* If you're going to be guillotined anyway, you might as well do it with spirit and dignity.

Why can't we have more colour in our lives? Take wireless licences. Must they be the colour of coffee with a dash of milk? They're like the paper used in prisons. You rather think you are being called up or getting a surtax demand owing since 1912.

If I were King for a Day I would wait for tomorrow before putting over reforms.

As I grow older – I'm forty-eight – I find that though I think I'm saying the same things as I always did, people listen to me more.

I never stand aside and look at myself in case I find out how I tick.

I haven't changed much in my attitude or opinions over forty years. It's just that I look older.

I am probably very happy because I am never content.

*　　*　　*

I would have liked to have met:

Sigmund Freud – but he would have made me shy.

Jesus Christ – but not till I've finished my play on Pontius Pilate.

Napoleon and *Hitler* – to have insulted them. I hate Napoleon, for he was no romantic. As for Hitler, he had vision but no insight.

Aristophanes and *Socrates* – just to have been amused.

*　　*　　*

Some brief definitions:

A sense of humour: Difficult to define in case you light on its mystery and destroy its innocence. But I would say that it's a readiness to see the funny side extant in everything.

A sense of the ridiculous: Thinking of the unfunny side of a situation first and then realising its funny side immediately afterwards.

A sense of comedy: To contrast a situation with its unfunny side.

A sense of the satirical: To recognise all the above and then bring it home swiftly to a third party.

*   *   *

Despite the many problems that his variegated professional commitments must create for him, Ustinov gives the impression of keeping enviably calm in most circumstances. In Love of Four Colonels *he perhaps offers the solution when a character says:*

A state of calm preserves your energy and enables you to go on being calm without undue effort.

*   *   *

Ustinov was asked how he relaxed:

I relax by going to bed and contemplating the ceiling. I would contemplate my navel like an Oriental mystic, only I can't see that far.

On Matters Military

When Ustinov was briefly attached to the War Office as a private, he wore an oversize topcoat, sewed up the badge of his cap unrecognisably, wore suède shoes, used a long cigarette holder and carried a swagger cane. Thus he shambled round London. He says:

I became a dab hand at accepting salutes most graciously, usually from bewildered Polish soldiers.

*　　　*　　　*

He told James Thomas of the Daily Express:

I am sure I would have been a howling success in the Army if I had been drafted as a general. But I never rose above 'Private, third class, smoking'.

*　　　*　　　*

Peter Ustinov has considerable sympathy for the plight of the Younger Generation. In his play Halfway Up The Tree *he makes a leading character say:*

What young people are really lacking is a Cause. It was

so easy for us. 'For King and Country', 'God is Love', 'Hang the Kaiser' – and with each one came an often unworthy simplification called duty, which covered a multitude of virtues.

What have they got?

The dissolution of the Empire is hardly compatible with 'For King and Country', Hiroshima is hardly compatible with God as the image of Love, while 'Hang the Kaiser' is hardly compatible with the fact that some friendly German tanks are at this moment holding summer exercises not twenty miles from here, as our guests.

* * *

From The Unknown Soldier and His Wife:

In war you know damn well that it is your sacred duty to kill the other fellow before you have time to find out if you have a common interest or not.

* * *

In a short story, Add A Dash Of Pity, *Ustinov makes a couple of derisory military points:*

An army officer remarks, 'I'm not allergic to stupidity. I'm amused by it. I'll probably end up a field-marshal.'

* * *

Ustinov admits that he was not a very accomplished soldier (and friends like David Niven sorrowfully confess that he was 'an utter shambles'), but proudly admits that there was war-like blood in his family. He cites the case of his Russian grandfather:

I had a Russian grandfather who, after a successful business career, emigrated to Palestine to become a missionary. By some oversight he failed to learn that his native Russia was at war with Germany until well into 1916. When he finally heard the news, although seventy-eight and scarcely able to walk, he went to the Russian Consulate in Jerusalem, brandishing a sword and carrying a written apology to the Czar for not having come to his rescue before.

* * *

From Halfway Up The Tree:

You talk like some ridiculous regimental officer. When in doubt let your sense of humour become frayed – when you haven't the brains to follow an argument, be on the safe side and accept an apology.

* * *

Film producer George Brown recalls when Private Ustinov had to visit a secret HQ in connection with an army film. A limousine arrived and the army chauffeur looked in horror at the horrible caricature of a soldier. 'You can't go to HQ like that,' he said, 'they'll put you on a charge.' Private Ustinov replied:

Thanks, corporal. Your badge is a bit cleaner than mine.

And he promptly swapped caps with the paralysed NCO.

* * *

Peter Ustinov's repugnance to war is vividly shown in a witty but bitter prayer rendered by the Archbishop in The Unknown Soldier and His Wife *to the God Mars:*

Let us pray. O Mighty Mars, Creator of Widows, fount of tears, lend us your ears in your infinite mercilessness and hear our prayers. Give us this day our daily victim and teach us to kill without compassion so that our civilising mission may go unhindered by cries of mercy or the yells of the despondent. Blind us to charity and deafen us to entreaty, for ever and ever, Amen.

* * *

On the dangers of dual nationality in times of war:

By German law I suppose I'm still German because my father was until he became British. I had a German passport till 1936, when I gave it up. It would have been tricky for me if I had been captured in the war by the Germans. They would not only have shot me for being a traitor but also clapped me in jail for failing to report with my call-up group.

* * *

Army traditions amuse this highly un-military wit:

125

One regiment wears one of the buttons of its tunic dented. Think of the man in the button-factory whose life's work was to dent the requisite buttons. One can almost hear St Peter's 'What was that?' at the pearly gates when an old man of startling purity described his life's vocation as 'button-denter'. It *is* a vocation. Such a man cannot have done less than to answer a call.

Paul I of Russia had a very short, degenerate nose, and so tradition took root that the yardstick for acceptance in his élite unit was not courage or height, but the shortness of a recruit's nose. It must have been a very neurasthenic regiment. Imagine walking in the morning to see a dormitory full of tiny noses just visible above the blankets, like submarines charging their batteries in hostile waters.

*   *   *

Ustinov apparently led a chequered military career:

A three-man selection board in the Army issued a daunting warning that in no circumstances should I be put in charge of other men. True to form, the Army obeyed that minor piece of advice to the letter.

Two weeks before I was demobilised I was put on guard duty in North London. I could never quite make out why the War Office apparently anticipated a final onslaught on Wembley's housewives from the German High Command.

I learned about colonels the hard way. I found they weren't at all bad when you get to know them, but opportunities for privates to get to know colonels are apt to be strictly limited.

In my early days in the Army I was always picked as a runner on exercises and had to charge all over huge fields delivering vital messages. They made me a runner because they assumed that, as an actor, I could remember long messages. But I was always so exhausted that I hadn't the breath to deliver the message. When I'd recovered my breath I'd forgotten it.

Four-and-a-half years in the British Army was the longest role I've ever played; grossly underpaid and I was miscast, but it was a big spectacular and a *very* long run.

*   *   *

But he formed some shrewd opinions:

I believe that generals detest generals on their own side far more than they dislike the enemy.

Most generals are damn bad writers, or at least show the same lack of discrimination in selecting their ghost-writers as they do in selecting their staff officers.

127

Technical achievements are now the order of the day. It is not so much lack of know-how which stands in the way of even smaller countries having their bombs or their missiles, but cash.

Have you noticed that bombs are called 'devices' when they don't explode?

*   *   *

He has never regarded himself as a Beau Brummell:

In my army uniform I looked like the loser in a sack-race.

A Letter from Grice

John Phillips, the actor who played in Peter Ustinov's Romanoff
and Juliet, *is one of many who cherish witty, nonsense letters
sent from Ustinov, usually when they were feeling low and
depressed. Phillips received many when he was in Rome suffering
from a swollen foot from the Italian heat. One day, says Phillips, I
thought it time to strike back. I wrote Peter a letter purporting to
come from a Professor Bate, a crabbed Oxford don who had
visited the studios and was now offering Ustinov a job as assistant
at his public lectures since he was 'good with properties'. I
mentioned a fee of two guineas. Next day came a reply. Peter
had become Arnold Grice BA (Aberystwyth), a sort of Welsh
Baron Corvo, cadging, cringing, boozing his way round the
world, eventually disappearing behind the Iron Curtain. The
character became more 3D and more desperate as the correspondence grew. He 'wrote' from The Three Bells, Leominster, from
the Vatican Library, from Leopoldville, from Moscow. But
wherever his 'lodging' Ustinov made Grice a very real character.
Here – at random – is Grice from Africa:*

Lycée César Franck,
81 Rue Emile Cammaerts,
Leopoldville

Bate!

Your vindictiveness knows no bounds! When you put pen to paper to liberate a heart charged with envy of its intolerable burden (for you have a conscience, Bate – cruelty does not come easily to you – nay, it has been acquired by many years of patient practice, and yet remaining a subject for which you have no natural aptitude – it takes its place by the side of humour in that respect) when you sat down in that unventilated, ivy-shrouded study of yours to write to me the report that the Chair of Mirth at Glastonbury, North Carolina, had been offered to Stephen Potter, who according to an article of the following day by Mr Holly Knickerbockers, married Mrs Julius Mendelssohn at a quiet ceremony at Grosse Point, attended by two thousand people with Mr E Power Biggs at the organ.

Bate, this you know, and yet feigned ignorance in order to give free flight to your poisonous barbs. I would not dream of accepting even one guinea from you, although if you could deposit ten shillings in the National Provincial Bank at Chepstow I would be more than grateful, since the negotiations with the Belgian Exchange Control are extremely protracted, and, although I began them through the good offices of the Reverend Father Huismans SJ, a really sound accountant out here, I have been forced by circumstances outside my control to begin all over again with a Watusi, Mr Basil M'Bowo, who has added to my difficulties by failing to understand that Chepstow is a town and not a Government Minister. If you do this I will overlook your habitual theft from *A Gull's Home Boke* (unacknowledged) during your Reith Lectures.

I really feel that I am doing some good here, among our

sombre friends, and the all-black *Othello*, in which I played the title role, drew applause from M Lumumba himself. Please send by return of post a can of 'Flit' and some mosquito netting – from the Army and Navy Stores. I will pay for it as soon as you have deposited the ten shillings in my bank.

> Yours faithfully,
>
> ARNOLD GRICE

PS. Webster has it that the plural of pamplemousse is pamplemice.

This, says Phillips, was Grice in full song. The correspondence cheered me up tremendously; and remember that, despite the many calls on his time, he found opportunity to give his fertile imagination yet another witty exercise.

Religion and the Church

As a man deeply concerned with civilisation Peter Ustinov has strong views about both the Church and religion, which are not necessarily the same. Some of his most sincere views are made more pungent by his witty attack, particularly on modern morals:

Things only become evil when they are no longer funny.

Pornography is a release rather than an encouragement. It is lack of imagination that makes people revel in pornography.

A twinge of conscience is a glimpse of God.

Religion is the work of God, perfected by the Devil.

Religion is superstition. It makes a man conscious of the alternatives.

Most of us are generally united by our doubts and divided by our convictions.

Priests – and politicians for that matter – should regard themselves as entertainers at least in so far that it's the entertainer's primary task to keep the audience awake.

It is becoming increasingly obvious that God is no longer with us. Up till now man has been tormented with questions to which there have been no answers; because of computers we are being showered with answers to which we have not even put the questions.

To understand is sometimes to love, sometimes to hate, always to forgive, always to enrich.

*   *   *

On capital punishment:

The death sentence is a misnomer. There is no death sentence; it is merely a sentence to spend the last days of life as unpleasantly as possible.

When the judge used to don his black cap with the words 'May God have mercy on your soul' he was extending his terms of reference into a territory in which he had no business.

*   *   *

Ustinov is intolerant of those who seek to put the world right by sheer force of rhetoric:

I

In order to complain about a tidal wave you have to be on more intimate terms with the Almighty than any mere mortal can be.

*   *   *

He is at present engaged in a play which will give a new slant on Pontius Pilate. He thinks that:

Pontius Pilate was not such a bad old baddie. He is much maligned. In the Coptic Church he is regarded as a saint, but theologians generally revile him. If they didn't they'd be out of a job.

*   *   *

He put many of his opinions on religion into his play The Unknown Soldier and His Wife, *always with wit blended with wisdom. Three times he crystallises the dogma of religion through his characters (but remember that he considers that the playwright must always be, also, the Devil's advocate):*

Religion is blackmail. It holds a man's opinion of himself to ransom.

On two occasions in his plays he holds up Church dignitaries to shrewd but gentle fun. In Romanoff and Juliet *he introduced an Archbishop with failing hearing with the comment:*

A deaf Archbishop can be a nuisance, but he may have his advantages. Of course, he only became Archbishop because he is entirely closed to the world of sound. It gave him an austerity which visibly enhanced his capacity for meditation.

*   *   *

Peter Ustinov wrote The Unknown Soldier and His Wife *because he felt that honouring an unknown warrior was simply an excuse for ducking the vital question of what causes war. He sums it up in a story he likes:*

A man visited Israel and asked to see the tomb of the Unknown Soldier. He was taken to a marble mausoleum near Tel Aviv and on it was carved: *Herman J Ginsberg (b 1883. d 1917)*.

He said: 'But I thought the soldier was supposed to be unknown?' The guide replied: 'As a soldier he was unknown – but as a *furrier* –!'

*   *   *

His play, Halfway Up The Tree, *has some pertinently witty comment on morals and religion of today:*

Temptation given in to promptly is no longer temptation. Temptation only comes with the second thought.

The General, in this play, remarks cynically:

I have found no vice that appeases me for longer than it takes to perform it.

The General also opines:

It is hard for a Christian to survive in a Godless society. The first casualty in a Godless society is always the Devil and without the Devil a Christian is lost.

General to the Vicar:

My soul is a matter between myself and God, and I'm quite willing to let you overhear the argument if you wish.

Vicar:

Your behaviour offers a most ticklish moral problem, simply because I can find no argument to condemn it.

VICAR: Where did you meet such a woman?
GENERAL: Outside a YWCA in London.
VICAR (*suspiciously*): On her way in or on her way out?

*   *   *

In Halfway Up The Tree *his stage directions describe the Vicar in the play as:*

A cavernous, dandruffy man with the fixed smile of a certain dangerous fish and a voice with an in-built echo.

It would be dangerous to assume, however, that this description sums up Ustinov's opinion of all vicars.

* * *

Actually, Peter Ustinov gets on well with men of the cloth as, in fact, he does with any man or woman who is not a proven fool. David Fairweather, the press manager of Chichester Festival Theatre, *and himself a man of wit, tells with glee how the Bishop of Reading visited the theatre for* The Unknown Soldier and His Wife *and Peter spotted him in the fourth row of the stalls, and later in the theatre restaurant. The Bishop wrote a warm letter to Ustinov congratulating him on the play and his performance as* The Archbishop, *adding 'You seemed a bit surprised on seeing me.' The ebullient Ustinov could not resist replying:*

I wasn't a bit surprised. Just startled to find someone else dressed like me.

* * *

From The Unknown Soldier and His Wife:

Doubts are the spurs of thoughts. The more I know what I am supposed to think the less I know what I really think.

* * *

And from Romanoff and Juliet:

There's nothing more suitable to announce your engagement to your friends than a nice religious postcard. It takes away all frivolous aspects of the negotiation, and has a spontaneous dignity which no amount of subsequent teasing can ever dispel.

Normal Service Will Be Resumed

Someone wrote to a newspaper to say that he would gladly pay treble the current cost of a television licence provided he had a guarantee that Peter Ustinov would appear for fifteen minutes a week 'doing precisely what he liked'. It was established that this sensible offer did not emanate from Ustinov himself. He is conscious of the urgent part that television plays in our lives, but he is alert to its responsibilities, its faults and its whimsicalities. He sums up television's impact with these cracks:

The only people who haven't appeared on television are those that are too busy watching it.

The sleepy salesman on an American commercial TV spot resembles an Arab vendor on a seashore eager to sell you an Axminster carpet, but more than delighted if you buy a collar stud.

Politicians are not taught to put themselves over on television. The more charming they are the less you believe. I remember once watching Harold Macmillan on the box. He kept looking at the camera as though it were a cobra.

He was appealing to the nation for calm and his face was frozen with terror.

The time's coming when politicians will be less concerned about equal time on television, but on equal billing.

When you are taking part in a television interview show the commercials always come on just as you are settling down and beginning to sound like Voltaire. I guarantee Voltaire wouldn't have stood for it.

I can't tolerate people who open a television or radio programme with the words: 'Good morning to you', as if they were personally dispensing one of God's miracles to you as a favour.

The great oracle of television bleats on unheeded in this world like a pianist in a crowded bar.

*   *   *

We see Peter Ustinov too little on British television, but he remembers, with mingled feelings, televising Peer Gynt:

I was tearing from studio to studio like a distraught Christmas Post Office volunteer worker trying to remember when Boxing Day falls.

Actor Robin Bailey remembers that occasion too. 'We were rehearsing for Peer Gynt *when the telephone rang for Peter. Without batting an eyelid he said:*

I'd better take it. It may be a troll call.

*   *   *

In Atlantic Monthly *Ustinov wrote:*

It is a curious phenomenon that in this glacial era of computers which we are just entering, it is warmth and warmth alone that succeeds on television.

*   *   *

He ponders on the impact on history if television had come earlier and wittily 'reviews' Adolf Hitler:

Had television existed in Hitler's day I doubt if he would have persuaded even the most hardened goose-stepping dolt that all was in order with the Reich. His fireside chat to the nation, in which he would presumably have been seated in an armchair near the burning Reichstag, might have begun in calm but would have swiftly disintegrated into an interminable harangue of the nation – and there is nothing more forbidding for the solitary viewer than to be addressed as though he were a huge cross-section of the populace.

*   *   *

Peter Ustinov is fascinated with America's television 'giveaway' shows. He says:

It is like watching medieval morality plays with all the vices paraded before you – particularly avarice.

*   *   *

He described BBC producer Pat Dixon as:

An extremely amiable and highly strung executive who looks like Beethoven in the throes of a great quartet.

*   *   *

From 'The Johnny Carson Show', 1965:

I particularly like one of the American automobile commercials. One gets the impression that if you go round in five minutes to a place forty-three miles away, you'll get a car for free.

In the same show Ustinov remarked:

I always thought that television would be a greater threat to politics than to movies or the theatre. And it's proved it. Now you've got people from our profession who suddenly don't see why they should help people with their make-up. Instead, they put it on themselves and run for office.

*   *   *

On British disc jockeys:

They try to deliver by intoning the lot in phoney New York accents that even New Yorkers stopped using about the time of prohibition. The extraordinary thing about it is that the American accent is out – even for Americans.

*   *   *

A make-up girl went to prepare him for an appearance in the David Frost show. She asked him how his make-up was. He ran his palms over his cheeks and replied, solemnly:

Isn't it all right? I put it on this morning as usual.

*   *   *

Character, to an Olympic Games miler, in Ustinov's play Halfway Up The Tree*:*

I've often admired you on television, but as I have only a very small screen and as you run so rapidly you've never been on it for very long.

*   *   *

Ustinov confesses:

In the States I appeared in the $64,000 Challenge programme and flunked at $8,000. I flopped on 'the exact location of the Shalimar Gardens'. The air-conditioning in my booth broke down and I came out, my ears popping, gasping for breath. I was preceded by a small, ten-year-old boy who used up all the air spelling very long words.

Acknowledgements

From memory, reading, conversation, watching his plays and from pestering many of his friends and colleagues I have gathered these thoughts and words of the wise, witty and irrepressible Peter Ustinov. Many people were unable to help and I share their regret and still thank them for their courteous effort. Others provided me with information, not suitable for this particular book, but which I hope will not be wasted in a further book on Ustinov.

But here are some to whom I am indebted and, if people have been omitted, I stand abashed.

Particularly I acknowledge the patient help of Peter Ustinov himself and of his charmingly co-operative secretary, Liliane Couturier and particularly for copies of some speeches he has made at high level.

I have drawn on items from the *Daily Express, Sunday Express, Evening Standard, Daily Mirror, Evening News, Daily Sketch, Sunday Telegraph, Daily Telegraph, Sunday Mirror, Atlantic Monthly, Time, Nova*, the now defunct *Illustrated, Homes and Gardens, Films and Filming*, and *Variety*. Transcripts of a BBC2 interview, a British Film Institute talk and an American television script kindly sent by Manny Reiser of *Four Seasons*, NY, through Tony Morris, were all most useful.

Press agents Paul Mills, Julian Senior and Bill Edwards of

ACKNOWLEDGEMENTS

MGM, Arthur Allighan of Walt Disney Productions and Rogers, Cowan & Brenner Inc were most helpful.

I acknowledge, gratefully, quotations from Geoffrey Willans' *Peter Ustinov* (Peter Owen, Ltd), and from a number of his plays, and his short stories, including *The Unknown Soldier and his Wife, Halfway Up The Tree, The Love of Four Colonels, The Indifferent Shepherd, Photo Finish, Romanoff and Juliet, Add A Dash Of Pity, The Loser*. My gratitude to the various publishers.

Finally, I acknowledge the help given by many individuals in supplying memories of Peter Ustinov's wit. They include, possibly not fully: Terence Stamp, Robin Bailey, David Nettheim, John Phillips, Alec Clunes, Walter Goetz, Moira Lister, Margot Lovell, Jessie Evans, Peter Jones, John Hunter of Film Rights, Robert Raglan, Eric Goodhead, David Fairweather, Bill and Phoebe Bevir, Diana Graves, George H Brown, David Niven, Mary Morris, Ferdy Mayne, Ian Keith, Molly Urquhart, Brenda and Roy Rich, Edward Hardwicke, Max Adrian, Paul Rogers, Charmain Eyre, David Lodge, Dennis Carey, Andrew Cruickshank, Colin Gordon, Ursula Jeans, Roger Livesey, Phil Algar, Joyce Grenfell and to Gallow for his caricature of Peter Ustinov in the prelims.

D R